Fat Mutton and Liberty of Conscience

FAT MUTTON AND LIBERTY OF CONSCIENCE

Society in Rhode Island, 1636-1690

CARL BRIDENBAUGH

Atheneum 1976 New York

To the memory of

RICHARD HARRISON SHRYOCK

1893–1972

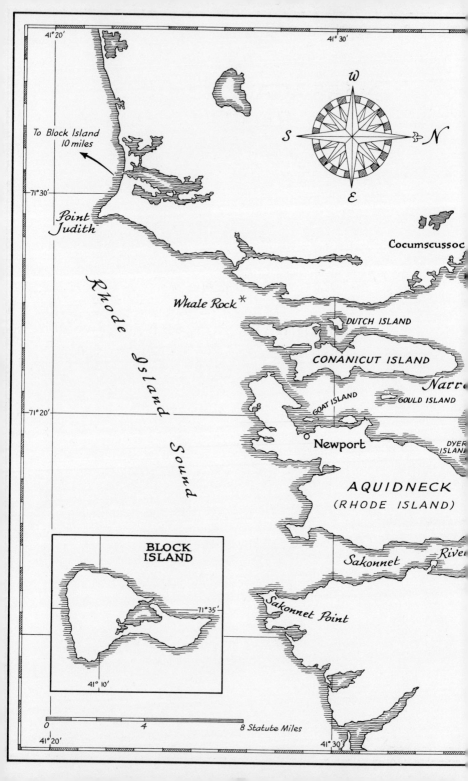

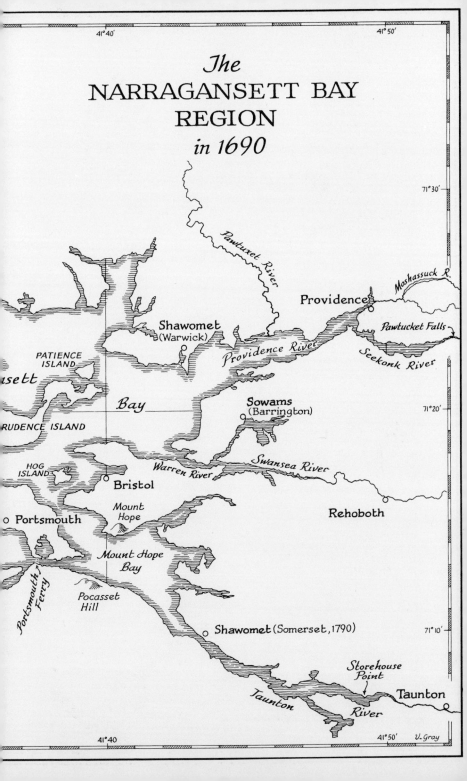

The
NARRAGANSETT BAY
REGION
in 1690

41°40'   41°50'

71°30'

Pawtuxet River

Providence
Moshassuck R.

Shawomet
(Warwick)
Pawtucket Falls

Providence River
Seekonk River

PATIENCE
ISLAND

...sett
Bay
Sowams
(Barrington)   71°20'

RUDENCE ISLAND

HOG
ISLAND
Warren River   *Swansea River*

Bristol

o Portsmouth
Mount
Hope
Rehoboth

Mount Hope
Bay

Portsmouth Ferry

*Pocasset
Hill*

Shawomet (Somerset, 1790)   71°10'

*Storehouse
Point*

Taunton
Taunton
River

41°40   41°50'   *U. Gray*

CONTENTS

List of Illustrations ix

A Note on the Sources xiii

Abbreviations Used in the Notes xv

Preface xix

I. The Mythical Rhode Island 3

II. Beginnings on Land and Sea 9

III. The Denizens of Naboth's Meadows 27

IV. The Quaker Grandees of Rhode Island 61

V. Agriculture Ushers in Commerce 93

Conclusion 127

Appendices

I. Landholding at Newport and Portsmouth, 1639–1640 133

II. George Fox's Letter to Rhode Island Officials, 1672 135

III. Rhode Island Merchants, 1636–1690 137

IV. Rhode Island Artisans and Tradesmen, 1638–1690 140

V. Early Whaling off Rhode Island, 1662 144

Index 149

LIST OF ILLUSTRATIONS

[*Between pages 40 and 41*]

Note: Any kind of pictorial material about seventeenth-century New England is hard to find, because very little was produced at the time, and of that but a fraction has survived. Hardly anything remains from early Rhode Island. Fortunately, farming books were popular in England and were often illustrated with engravings that portrayed domestic animals which, although of shapes and sizes much different from those of today, were familiar sights on the islands and shores of Narragansett Bay.

Endpapers. THE NARRAGANSETT BAY REGION IN 1690

Plate 1. AN ENGLISH BARNYARD, 1675

Although the background of this scene differs markedly from that of a contemporary New England farm, most of the barns erected in Rhode Island and Providence Plantations closely resembled the one pictured here. The absence of windows or openings for air was compensated for by the loose-fitting siding of fir or pine deals. A small lean-to has been added, indicating that this structural device was English rather than colonial in origin. Entry for men, horses, and carts was through the projecting gable porch on the long side of the barn; the portal was closed by two great batten doors. The four-wheeled cart of hay is being drawn by three beasts harnessed in tandem rather than as a team. All of the cattle shown have very long horns. From a detail in the bottom-left corner of the frontispiece engraved by F. H. Van Houe for John Worlidge, *Systema Agriculturae* (London, 1675). Courtesy of the Library Company of Philadelphia.

Plate 2. HUSBANDMEN AT WORK, 1685

Beginning at the upper left and proceeding clockwise, the vignettes depict: (1) plowing, (2) sowing and angling, (3) harrowing the soil, (4) making a stake-and-withe fence, (5) treating a sick ox, (6) driving a two-wheeled cart—the usual Rhode Island vehicle, (7) cutting grain with a sickle, (8) harvesting with a scythe, (9) beekeeping, (10) transplanting a fruit tree. The smocks, short trousers, and heavy socks worn by the English husbandmen were costumes commonly seen in the earliest days of settlement, before the wearing of deerskin garments and leggings became habitual with the Rhode Islanders. From Joseph Blagrave, *The Epitome of the Whole Art of Husbandry* (London, 1685), frontispiece. Courtesy of the Library Company of Philadelphia.

Plate 3. A RHODE ISLAND STONE-ENDER, 1687

The Eleazer Arnold House in Lincoln, Rhode Island, built in 1687, is the best-preserved seventeenth-century structure in Rhode Island. Originally it had a high-peaked front gable; the rear roof line was raised when the second room was added. The massive fireplaces with the impressive stack were characteristic of the colony, where ample fieldstone and lime were available. A plan of a stone-ender with a lean-to added, together with Norman Isham's drawing of the first form of the Arnold House, may be found in Hugh Morrison, *Early American Architecture* (New York, 1952), figures 48–50, pages 66–67. Photograph by courtesy of the Rhode Island School of Design.

Plate 4. THE SILVER FLEECE OF NEWPORT

As far as is now known, this is the only representation in existence of any living thing of seventeenth-century Rhode Island. It is also the earliest work in silver of the colony, having been fashioned by Arnold Collins about 1696. From it we discover that the ovines of the Narragansett region were long legged, with unusually long tails, and that their fleeces were not as thick and heavy as those of present-day American sheep, which are descended from the Merino strain. The lettering of the seal reads: COUNCEL SEAL OF NEWPORT RHOADE ISLAND. Photographed by John Hopf and reproduced by the courtesy of the custodian, the Newport Historical Society.

A NOTE ON THE SOURCES

THE historian has a duty to pay the strictest attention to chronology; in writing on economic and social life, proper chronology is absolutely vital. This obligation should be made clear to the reader at once. Too often in the writing of early American history, the tendency has been to lump the seventeenth and eighteenth centuries together, as though what was true of the years 1607–90 would also be true from 1690 to 1775, and especially vice versa. Obviously this never was true. Change is the essence of economic and social history. In the present work, with a single exception, no source has been used that dates beyond 1690. This point is stressed to avoid misunderstanding.

For the years 1607–90, the economic and social materials are more abundant than one might anticipate, and from them can be extracted answers to many questions not previously posed about life in Rhode Island during the seventeenth century. On the other hand, the sources for the period before 1690 are fewer and more scanty in content than those for the nine succeeding decades. There are many pertinent questions which twentieth-century readers will ask to which no answers can be given. A few examples may illustrate the difficulty. Statistics on population do not exist, so estimates must serve. And, because the number of Negro slaves was so small, any inquiry about slave labor on the plantations at Narragansett or on Rhode Island itself is relevant only to the eighteenth century. There is no evidence of the exporting of flax or linsey-woolsey cloth. Two matters were of great concern in the writing of this book: the first was to discover the number, tonnage, and types of ships belonging to Narragansett Bay; the second was to obtain some measurement of the total wealth of the inhabitants and the range of its distribution. To these and many similar questions there is just no answer in the documents, and one has to be thankful for what he can find in them.

An extensive bibliographical comment about the sources used in the preparation of this book seems unnecessary, for they are well known to students of the history of Rhode Island. Most of them can be found in the Rhode Island Historical Society and the Rhode Island Archives in the State House, both at Providence, or in the Newport Historical Society, Touro Street, Newport. That these repositories yielded as much material for the subject as they did, despite great gaps in the record, suggests that discoveries of the same nature may be made in other archives of New England. No one could have been more surprised than the writer by the story revealed in the research and writing, and the unanticipated conclusions reached in this study.

ABBREVIATIONS USED

IN THE NOTES

Short Titles

Aspinwall Recs.	*Aspinwall Notarial Records from 1644 to 1651*, 32d Report of the Record Commissioners of the City of Boston (Boston, 1903)
CSM Pubs.	Colonial Society of Massachusetts, *Publications*
Doc. Hist. R.I.	*Documentary History of Rhode Island*, ed. Howard M. Chapin (2 vols., Providence, 1916)
MHS Colls.	Massachusetts Historical Society, *Collections*
MHS Procs.	Massachusetts Historical Society, *Proceedings*
Narr. Club Pubs.	"Letters of Roger Williams," *Narragansett Club Publications*, VI (Providence, 1874)
NEQ	*New England Quarterly*
Portsmouth Recs.	*The Early Records of the Town of Portsmouth*, ed. Clarence S. Brigham (Providence, 1901)
Providence Recs.	*Early Records of the Town of Providence*, ed. W. C. Pelky (21 vols., Providence, 1892–1915)

R.I. Col. Recs.	*Records of the Colony of Rhode Island and Providence Plantations*, ed. John R. Bartlett (10 vols., Providence, 1856–65)
RIHS Colls.	Rhode Island Historical Society, *Collections*
RIHS, MSS	Rhode Island Historical Society, Manuscripts
R.I. Land Evidences	Rhode Island Land Evidences, 1646–1708, manuscript transcript (Rhode Island Historical Society), I
R.I. Land Evidences	*Rhode Island Land Evidences: Abstracts* (Providence, 1921), I (1648–96)
Sanford Letter Book	*The Letter Book of Peleg Sanford of Newport, Merchant . . . 1666–1668* (Providence, 1928)
Stevens, Transcripts	Henry F. Stevens, comp., Historical Manuscripts from H.B.M. State Paper Office, 1618–1735 (9 vols., transcripts, John Carter Brown Library)
Winthrop Papers	*Winthrop Papers* (5 vols., Massachusetts Historical Society, Boston, 1929–)
Winthrop's Journal	*Winthrop's Journal: "History of New England," 1630–1649*, ed. James K. Hosmer, in *Original Narratives of Early American History*, ed. J. Franklin Jameson (2 vols., New York, 1908)

Libraries and Archives

JCB	John Carter Brown Library, Providence
Mass. Archives	Massachusetts Archives, State House, Boston

MHS	Massachusetts Historical Society, Boston
NHS	Newport Historical Society
R.I. Archives	Rhode Island Archives, State House, Providence
RIHS	Rhode Island Historical Society, Providence

PREFACE

AMERICAN historians are all city slickers. And so often, as Royall Tyler first depicted Jonathan in *The Contrast* in 1787, they turn out to be far more naïve about life in the past than the knowledgeable hayseed, who now has vanished, leaving behind only spurious country music. Scholars today, and many of their mentors, are unconsciously limited and misdirected by their environment and upbringing. They attended city schools and most of them got their advanced training at city universities, where they studied and researched almost exclusively in the great libraries. Little they saw in Nature that was theirs. God is said to be dead, everywhere; and one looks with dismay, frequently with horror, at what man has done to the town.

The neophytes of the historical profession—and some others too—do not realize that the primary fact about our colonial past was the ruralness of America, a condition which determined that agriculture, in its widest sense, would be the daily activity of virtually all its people—even of the ministry. Yet so pervasive are modern urban influences that students today, those from the countryside included, have not the slightest insight into what this meant or how much different the seventeenth century was from the twentieth. Further, most of the research and publication of the past three decades dealing with the colonial period has been on topics that, however novel or fresh, are peripheral rather than central to the subject. Urban ignorance has been causing historians to misunderstand and seriously distort the first half of American history. It is not that they have forgotten what the past was really like; rather it is that they have never known.

If the truth about the past is not to remain either unknown or misunderstood, and our youthful historians are not to be kept in outer darkness concerning rural and agricultural life, what are the "needs and opportunities" to which teachers of and writers on early American history ought to address themselves?

It may seem paradoxical for one whose principal role as a writer of history has been to emphasize the significance of urban life in the colonial period suddenly to face about like a weathercock and call his fellows in the guild back to the farm. Yet in *Cities in the Wilderness* (1938) and in the books that followed it colonial urban development was analyzed and described against the then familiar background and placed in the setting of the entire Western World. Today, conditions are different. The great obligation of our time is not for the historians to single out one thread or a neglected fragment of the past but to recover and reconstruct the whole of colonial history before it disappears, perhaps for eternity. How can this be done?

Early American history was also a very significant part of contemporary English history, which in turn was a segment of the history of the Western World. The European agricultural-industrial-commercial system, and that of England especially, developed slowly out of the later Middle Ages. The expansion of the people of the British Isles to North America and the Caribbean during the seventeenth and eighteenth centuries produced a sea change, one that forced unperceived modifications of the civilization in transit. If one assumes that Jacobean and Caroline England (1607–1649) represented equilibrium, then, from the outset, in Virginia, Bermuda, the islands of the West Indies, and New England, this equilibrium either became unstable or began rapidly to collapse. A disintegrating equilibrium requires immediate action, and in many instances, conservatism as an attitude has to be abandoned or, at least, dispensed with temporarily. To survive and prosper under wilderness conditions, some men have to take new and often radical measures in order to fit their old institutions and customs, even their very selves, into novel and strange surroundings.

An overwhelming majority of the English immigrants to this hemisphere before 1690 were either husbandmen or yeomen—agriculturalists—and they came here to get land and be farmers. At once, however, the colonists met Nature in a strange new guise. The climate of the new lands was either hotter or colder than that of England; and rainfall was either abundant or sparse. Everything appeared to be extreme rather than moderate. Before they could begin to farm as they had planned so optimistically, they found that they must prepare land for cultivation, cut down great trees or clear out dense underbrush (or both), and then either kill off or drive away predatory and destructive wild animals. This they accomplished only to face the unanticipated problem of soils, fertile and barren, inasmuch as they knew nothing of the science of agronomy. To put it another way, the agricultural technology of the migrating English was unsuited for the American wilderness; it had to be radically altered and revised, much of it even discarded; and new skills (such as handling an ax) had to be learned, and new methods worked out.

There were other aspects of agriculture with which the colonists had to deal from the very first. There was the land itself: how would it be parceled out and to whom? What should be the size of the holdings, and the method of tenure? Final answers to these and other fundamental questions were not forthcoming in most regions and plagued the settlers throughout the seventeenth century. Matters concerning seeds, livestock, draft animals, vegetable gardening, proper manuring, suitable tools, various winter and summer chores, fencing, carts, roadways, and a host of similar concomitants of general farming inevitably turned out to be very different from what the settlers had been used to in England.

The practice of agriculture in the new world encompassed all human activities, the most obvious being provision for adequate housing, ample labor, apprenticeship, and education; for roads, bridges, and ferries; for auxiliary crafts and industries; for merchants, mariners, and markets; for wharves, warehouses, and ships. And at the same time all political and legal institutions from the town meeting to the Parliament, relations with other colonies, with the Crown, and with foreign nations demanded consideration by the settlers. Above and beyond all else was the matter of acceptable ways of worshipping God. It must be plain that coping with all these affairs, in addition to the unforeseen obstacles to planting, cultivating, and harvesting, called for men who were resilient and resourceful.

The central theme of early American history is to be found in the nature and achievements (or failures) of an agricultural-commercial society. This society is the matrix in which were formed, and from which issued, the ideas, faiths, ideals, and daily attitudes of the people, just as it was concurrently the central theme of the history of Western Europe. If today's *Weltanschauung* is characterized as industrial, then most certainly that of the Western World of the seventeenth and eighteenth centuries must be recognized as agricultural.

In seeking ways to understand, analyze, and describe in human terms what the colonial agricultural experience meant to those individuals who spent their lives under its profound influence, the historian must not confine either his thinking or his teaching and writing to planting, cultivating, and harvesting. He is charged with the responsibility of treating a central theme of infinite complexity, one intertwined with or comprehending every other phase of the life of that time—whether contemplative or active. Any other kind of history ends up as little more than a technical exercise.

The historian's problem is to discover and apply ways and means for dealing with such an intricate subject, and then to begin anew by working from the sources, whence he will derive his facts and draw exciting new ideas. He will have to frame all kinds of new questions to ask of his sources and be constantly on the alert to recognize new, occasionally strange, and different relationships between and among facts. In doing this, he will naturally employ such devices and methods as are required for enlightenment, not just those that are fashionable at the moment or convenient substitutes for clear thinking and felicitous exposition.

The quest of the scholar for new information and his reflections upon what he has uncovered will lead him far beyond the limits of inquiry into a single topic or thread of history. Nothing is lost when he becomes learned, however, for wide learning is what historians need today more than anything else. The field of American history to 1790 is not so vast that one curious man, by dint of persistence, ranging reading, and hard thought cannot come very close to encompassing it in a lifetime. Thereby he may achieve a complete perspective, a whole view of one of the great periods of history, and thus a more accurate understanding of the past.

One is always governed, yea restrained and restricted, by the sources available to him. Sometimes they are unexpectedly rich and yield readily to the asking of new questions; at other times they are meager, as, for example, about farm labor in New England or about selective breeding of livestock. On occasion the sources tell nothing at all. But the archives are full of such unexplored materials as court and land records. Moreover the old published collections can prove amazingly valuable when they are reread for other than political or institutional facts.

Agriculture in colonial Rhode Island has never had a chronicler. For this region, before 1700 at least, a wealth of evidence demonstrates that the growth of an agricultural-commercial society, in some ways unique, is the central theme of its history. If perchance the path to understanding early American history taken in this book should lead one or more historians to write similarly about the other New England communities or the largely unstudied Middle Colonies, the author will have achieved his purpose. In any event, one hopes that it may stand as an example of local history sketched on a broader canvas than earlier accounts and make local and provincial histories illuminate the entire scene of English history—not just Rhode Island and Providence Plantations but all of New England, and the English Caribbean colonies and the Mother Country as well.

F o r generously sharing with me their knowledge of Rhode Island books and records, Albert T. Klyberg, Nathaniel N. Shipton, and Noel P. Conlon have my warmest thanks. On March 18, 1973, the Trustees and Officers of the Rhode Island Historical Society made me the first Fellow of their venerable organization. On that occasion I read a paper based upon materials taken from the present study, and I acknowledge gratefully the helpful comments made by several of the members. I am also indebted to Mrs. Peter Bolhouse of the Newport Historical Society, and to Mr. Edwin Wolf II and Miss Stefanie Munsing of the Library Company of Philadelphia, as well as to Mrs. Marjorie Colt of the Rhode Island School of Design for much-needed help with the illustrations. In many ways, as always, Roberta Bridenbaugh has contributed to this book.

C a r l   B r i d e n b a u g h

Providence
24 September 1973

FAT MUTTON

AND LIBERTY OF

CONSCIENCE

I

THE MYTHICAL

RHODE ISLAND

HISTORY, like Nature, abhors a vacuum; where facts about the past are lacking, the story is promptly pieced out with fancy. Nowhere in the history of the English colonies in North America during the seventeenth century is this truth more clearly reflected than in early Rhode Island and Providence Plantations.

In the summer of 1657, a ship carrying a party of Quakers was sent away from New Amsterdam. Evidently greatly relieved, two dominies of the Reformed Dutch Church, Johannes Megapolensis and Samuel Drisius, wrote to Holland that, in all probability, the Friends had sailed to Rhode Island, "for that is the receptacle of all sorts of riff-raff people, and is nothing else than the sewer [their Latin reads *latrina*] of New England. All the cranks of New England retire thither."[1]

Unsympathetic or hostile chroniclers harped upon this noisome figure of the sewer throughout the seventeenth century—and long after. One of them spoke of the Quakers as "the Saints Errant," and another of Rhode Island as "the Island of Error." The Anglican John Josselyn noted that the settlement was "uncharitably called Rogue Island" by the Bostoners. And, never to be outdone, the Reverend Cotton Mather referred in the *Magnalia Christi Americana* of 1702 to "the giddy sectaries of this Island." Over the line to the west in Killingworth, a Connecticut parson, John Woodbridge,

1. Edward T. Corwin, comp., *Ecclesiastical Records of the State of New York* (Albany, 1901), I, 399–400.

Jr., described vividly, but without Christian compassion, for Richard Baxter in England "the Mold and manners of our Churches in this wilderness," including "if 'tis not too sluttish to be handled," the island of Aquidneck:

"Road Island is a chaos of all Religions and like materia prima susceptive of all formes. Sir Henry Moodyes short description of it is merry yet true and apt, that at Road Island there is enough of 2 good things, Fat Mutton and Liberty of Conscience. It is the Asylum for all that are disturbed for Heresy, a hive of hornets, and the Sinke into which all the Rest of the Colonyes empty their Hereticks. So that the body of the people are an Heterogeneous Lump of Familists, Antinomians, Quakers, Seekers, and Antisabbatarians. The best Limb in it is a church of Anabaptists led by Mr. [John] Clarke who they say is an Animal Rationale, of Competent Abilityes and Morall principles, but ever duo gladii he is both a magistrate and a Teacher: I will not say Elder for they hold no such office. As for the rest, or at least the Generality of them, they neither owne nor Attend any Sacrament. There is a small Town called Providence (if the name be not too sacred for the Thing) upon the Maine[land] ... (the Nest of that fallen Star Mr. [Roger] Williams whose name I presume is not unknown to you) containing about 40 or 50 Householders, though so small yet tripartited into 3 distinct Churches and Congregations each differing from [the] other in their principles. And the whole Jurisdiction, if they agree in any one position, [it] is this, That every Man though of any Hedge religion ought to professe and practice his own tenets without any molestation or disturbance."[2]

At this point one may properly inquire, What kind of an image had the colonists formed of themselves, fugitives from religious

2. "It is full of people haveing been a receptacle for people of severall Sorts and Opinions," Samuel Maverick wrote in 1660. *MHS Procs.*, 2d ser., I, 243; *MHS Colls.*, 3d ser., III, 316; Cotton Mather, *Magnalia Christi Americana* (Hartford, 1853), II, 520, 523; John Woodbridge, Jr., to Richard Baxter, March 31, 1671, in *NEQ*, X, 572–73.

persecution that they were? In 1652 Dr. John Clarke pointed out in *Ill Newes from New-England* that "notwithstanding the different understandings and consciences amongst us, without interruption we agree to maintain civil Justice and judgement; neither were there such outrages committed mongst us as in other parts of the Country are frequently seen." Two years later, in answer to Sir Henry Vane's question: "How is it that there are such divisions amongst you?" Gregory Dexter replied from Providence that the people of Rhode Island and Providence Plantations have been "sitten quiet and drie from the streams of blood spilt by the [Civil] warr in our native country . . . nor (in this colonie) have we been consumed with the over-zealous fire of the Godly and Christian magistrates."[3]

This same Doctor Clarke astutely petitioned King Charles II to allow the struggling and threatened colony to become a "flourishing civill State . . . with a full liberty in religious government," because "true pyety grounded upon gospell principles will give the best and greatest security to true soveraignty. . . ." It is well known that the Merry Monarch acceded graciously to this shrewd plea with the unprecedented religious clause of the Charter of 1663, which, in an age of faith, legitimated the first secular state of modern times.[4]

It is not for the author or his readers at this late date to take sides either with Rhode Island or her traducers. The magistrates of the four United Colonies and those other New Englanders whose unchristian actions threatened the very existence of these plantations accepted sincerely and without reservation the claim that there was but one true church and that that church was the Congregational, or New England Way. Beware of "such as do a toleration hatch," Governor Thomas Dudley taught. Toleration, let alone religious liberty, had no authorization from the Holy Scriptures; it was

3. John Clarke, *Ill Newes from New-England* (London, 1652), sig. A-4; *R.I. Col. Recs.*, I, 285, 288.
4. *R.I. Col. Recs.*, I, 490–91; II, 4–6.

simply alien to the "Puritan Mind," and when the Quakers made Rhode Island their base for proselyting and invaded the United Colonies, fear, as it usually does, triumphed over reason and humanity. Certain men of Massachusetts Bay exemplified the Reverend John Cotton's oft-repeated comment that "some men are all church, and no Christ."[5]

Fear of heresies, concern about the very foundations of the Puritan state, can be understood though not condoned; but naked greed cloaked in the guise of the faith we can neither condone nor even comprehend. It had about it the pungent odor of hypocrisy. There is no lack of evidence that some of the neighbors of the Rhode Islanders, especially in Massachusetts (if we may phrase it in biblical terms they would have recognized at once), coveted NABOTH'S MEADOWS, for it was on their grass that Sir Henry Moody discovered the second good thing about this tiny colony of outcasts—FAT MUTTON. From 1630 to 1690 the political leaders, the clergy, and not a few of the richer inhabitants of Massachusetts Bay, Plymouth, and Connecticut sincerely and devoutly believed and acted as if, annually, the Lord God had proclaimed an open season for them to prey upon all Rhode Islanders and seize their fruitful lands on the islands or along the shores of Narragansett Bay.[6]

5. Thomas Hutchinson, *History of the Colony and Province of Massachusetts-Bay*, ed. Lawrence S. Mayo (Cambridge, 1936), I, 67n.; Mather, *Magnalia*, I, 500.

6. The first instance, and a most transparent one, of specious reasoning by the men of Massachusetts who coveted lands to the southward involves Governor John Winthrop, who wrote in 1642: "At this court also, four of Providence, who could not consort with Gorton and that company, and therefore were continually injured and molested by them, came and offered themselves and their lands, etc., to us, and were accepted under our government and protection. This we did partly to rescue these men from unjust violence, and partly to draw in the rest in those parts, either under ourselves or Plymouth, who now lived under no government, but grew very offensive, and the place was likely to be of use to us, especially if we should have occasion

Virtually every one of the New England colonists was a puritan—with a little *p* that is. They all agreed that it was their duty to follow diligently their divinely ordained callings in this life and that God signified His approval of the industrious elect by guiding them along the way to wealth. Did not the familiar old English proverb teach that God helps them who help themselves? In this respect the Saints at the Bay and in Connecticut were in rare accord with the "heretics" of Rhode Island: the Winthrops, father and son, saw eye to eye with William Coddington and Roger Williams. Wherever he dwelt, the puritan was always quite as much concerned about coping with "the long littleness of life" as he was in examining the present state of his soul and the promise of the hereafter.

Both contemporary and subsequent historians who have written about New England (including several from Rhode Island) have persistingly denigrated Rhode Island and Providence Plantations by stretching the "receptacle" theory of religious multiplicity to embrace every other aspect and activity of the colony during the seventeenth century. They have misunderstood and greatly exaggerated political divisions; they have overlooked the existence of an orderly population with a genuine respect for English law and Christian morality by condemning, often in florid prose, far fewer lapses than they could have readily uncovered at Boston or New Haven at the same time; and they have insisted erroneously that education was totally neglected and the people left illiterate and therefore barbarous. In short, they have tended to see early Rhode

---

of sending out against any Indians of Naragansett and likewise for an outlet into the Naragansett Bay, and seeing it came without our seeking, and would be no charge to us, we thought it not wisdom to let it slip." *Winthrop's Journal*, II, 81. One of the "four of Providence" was William Arnold, who remarked cogently of the banishing of Samuel Gorton from Plymouth: "I say, there is no State but in the first place will seek to preserve its owne safety. . . ." Quoted by Edward Winslow, *Hypocrisie Unmasked* (London, 1646), 61.

Island as the sewer for all kinds of human, political, social, and economic, as well as religious, refuse. Although no contemporary said it, the impression was given that in the dreadful times at the end of the world, Rhode Island would be hell.[7]

The founding of a colony on Narragansett Bay, it must be made clear at the outset, was an almost accidental occurrence: one either of mere chance or, as the Puritans viewed it, the act of an angry God. The stubborn idealism of Roger Williams started it all in 1636, and two years later the willful mysticism of Anne Hutchinson furthered it and ensured its permanence. Irreconcilable religious differences set in motion a large migration of rejected Saints from Massachusetts Bay, and by 1644 Governor John Winthrop could confide to his journal that the island of Aquidneck alone sheltered "above 120 families," which suggests that the population was nearly 1,000.[8]

The prime fact about religion in Rhode Island and Providence Plantations was the absence of a priesthood, or hierarchy, which permitted the growth of a secular state, the expansion of settlement, and the development of a laissez-faire economy. This is but a fragment of the complete story, however, the mere outline of a tale that must be told with a wealth of facts and as little conjecture as possible.

7. For schools at Newport before 1690, see Carl Bridenbaugh, *Cities in the Wilderness: The First Century of Urban Life in America, 1625–1742* (New York, 1938), 123; and, for example, the existence of a schoolhouse in Warwick as early as 1653, *Early Records of the Town of Warwick*, ed. Howard M. Chapin (Providence, 1926), 75; and *Providence Recs.*, I, 40; III, 35; XV, 83.

8. Thomas Lechford reported 200 families on Aquidneck in 1642, which, at 8 persons to a family, would make 1,600 inhabitants, or thereabouts. Governor Winthrop was probably closer to the truth. "Plain Dealing," in *MHS Colls.*, 3d ser., III, 96; *Winthrop's Journal*, II, 175.

II

BEGINNINGS ON

LAND AND SEA

THE founding, settlement, survival, and successful growth and development of the Colony of Rhode Island and Providence Plantations as a flourishing society between 1632 and 1690 was the outcome of the juxtaposition and, ultimately, the combining of several elements, which have never before been treated as a complete whole. Puritanism has too long clouded over other equally fundamental matters in the history of early Rhode Island, which can be understood only in its complex entirety.

First and always present was the physical scene for this drama in which men and women strove to create a new, better, and safer life for themselves and their progeny. In the Narragansett Bay region, the English settlers came into contact with a markedly different natural environment from that which they had known previously, either in Old England or at the Bay Colony or Plymouth. (See endpapers.) Water, water, everywhere! No matter where they located—Providence, Pawtuxet, Portsmouth, Newport, Warwick—they could look out on the great bay with its islands and the several rivers leading some distance inland, such as the Moshassuck, Seekonk, Warren, and Taunton. These were unrivaled, protected waters containing a superb harbor and a spacious roadstead. Here might be had varieties of edible fish, bivalves, and crustaceans in great abundance. And close by lay Rhode Island Sound, its lanes opening on the east to Martha's Vineyard and around Cape Cod to Boston, as well as westward to Connecticut, Long Island, and Manhattan.[1]

The colonizing of the New World by the Europeans was, in fact, above everything else one vast maritime enterprise. Throughout the colonial era, a salty quality was never lacking, and this was especially true of the seaboard settlements of seventeenth-century New England. Early in the 1620's, the Dutch of New Netherland began to sail in their shallops up Long Island Sound to traffic with the Indians of Narragansett, and, after 1625, they used the base that Abraham Pietersen had erected for the West India Company on "Quetenis, lyeing in Sloop Bay" and later known as Dutch Island. Some of these Hollanders crossed Narragansett Bay to Sowams (Barrington) in 1632 and warned Captain Myles Standish of Plymouth that the Pequot tribe had grown overly hostile to the friendly Narragansetts. Captain William Peirce returned to Boston two years later in the Medford-built *Rebecca* (40 tons) with five hundred bushels of much-needed maize; it had been procured from the Narragansetts by the enterprising John Oldham and assembled on Prudence Island, which the Indians had recently given to him.[2]

Although both Roger Williams and Mistress Anne Hutchinson led small bands overland to their respective refuges, the large majority of the exiles sailed with their goods and animals around Cape Cod in small vessels—pinnaces and shallops—to their new homes, for as yet no roads led from Massachusetts Bay to the Narragansett shores. One can say that Roger Williams led an amphibious existence from his first days at Seekonk as he paddled

1. Settlements on Narragansett Bay

1636	Providence	1639	Newport
1637	Cocumscussoc ("Narragansett")	1643	Shawomet (Warwick)
1638	Pawtuxet	1657	Conanicut
1638	Portsmouth		

2. *A Treatise of New England published Ann. Dom. 1637* (Reprinted, London [?] before 1650, in Ebeling Collection, Houghton Library, Harvard University), 14; John R. Brodhead, *History of the State of New York* (New York, 1853), I, 268; *RIHS Colls.*, XIX, 90; *Winthrop's Journal*, I, 79, 111, 138.

to and fro on the bay and its tributaries in his great dugout canoe;
by 1637, when he was purchasing the Providence lands from the
natives, he had acquired two larger vessels. He complained to
Governor Winthrop about the demands of Canonicus and his fel-
lows for services of many sorts: "They had my son, my shallop and
Pinnace and hired servant etc., at command on all occasions. Trans-
porting 50 at a Time and Lodging 50 at a Time in my house." On
the other hand, the accommodating chief laid out for his host
"Grounds for a trading house at Nahiganset with his own hands."
Writing again to Winthrop a year later about their joint ownership
of Prudence Island, Williams informed the governor: "I have a
lustie Canow and shall have occasion to runn downe often to the
Iland (neere 20 mile from us) both with mine owne, and (I desire
allso freely) your worships swine. . . ."[3]

When the first settlers reached Pocasset, or Portsmouth, on
Aquidneck Island in 1638, not only had local shipping in small
craft developed on Narragansett Bay, but the excellent harbor at
the southern end of the island had already won an intercolonial
reputation as a port of call for coastal traffic. Nearly six months
before the migrants from Portsmouth named their settlement at
the southern end of Aquidneck, Roger Williams reported from
Providence on December 30: "I heare of a pinnace to put in to
Newport bound for Virginia." About a month later, Williams
sailed around Point Judith in one of his ships and up the Pequot
(Thames) River to "Monhiggin" (as Norwich was then called) to
visit Uncas, the sachem of the Mohegans.[4]

3. After the murder of John Oldham in his pinnace near Block Island
by the Indians of that place in 1636, Prudence Island was sold by Miantonomo
and Canonicus to Roger Williams and Governor Winthrop for two coats
and twenty fathoms of wampum. *Doc. Hist. R.I.*, I, 26, 47–48; Samuel G.
Arnold, *History of the State of Rhode Island and Providence Plantations*
(New York, 1859), I, 87; *Winthrop's Journal*, I, 264, 273–74; *Winthrop
Papers*, IV, 7.

4. May 16, 1639: "It is Agreed and ordered, that the Plantacon now begun

The founders of Newport set out by boat from Portsmouth in May 1639. William Coddington led the way thither in his own pinnace and, within seven months, dispatched it to Block Island with some livestock to be left there to graze. In after years William Cooley recalled how, "being Master of a boat," he and his crew of two stopped en route to put Mr. William Dyer ashore to take possession of a small island, which has borne his name ever since.[5]

When the vast extent of the Atlantic seaboard and its hinterland as far as the Appalachians is considered, the tiny colony of religious refugees seems to be no more than a spot on the map. We are admittedly investigating a comparatively small area, one composed of the present state of Rhode Island from the Pawcatuck to the Sakonnet River on the south and northward to the Massachusetts line. It also included the valley lands up the Seekonk River beyond the falls, the Warren River to Rehoboth, and the Taunton as far as the limits of navigation, Storehouse Point in the present town of Dighton. (See endpapers.)

The most striking geographical feature of the district is the great expanse of Narragansett Bay, whose waters occupy more than half of this region, but we shall concern ourselves principally with its roomy islands: Hog, Patience, Prudence, Dyer, Gould, Goat, Conanicut, and Dutch, as well as Aquidneck, or Rhode Island itself. The entire area included some five thousand acres of rich silt loam and more than seventy thousand acres fit for general farming and apple orchards, and excellent for grazing.

In the first report the Puritans of Massachusetts Bay received, Captain Peirce stated that "The country on the west of the Bay of Naragansett is all champaign for many miles, but very stony, and full of Indians." Much of the best farm land was located on the islands or along the western shores of the bay, which, in places, had been cleared about eight miles inland, for as soon as the natives

att this South west end of the Island shall be called Newport. . . ." *Doc. Hist. R.I.*, II, 71; *Winthrop Papers*, IV, 88; *R.I. Col. Recs.*, I, 45.

5. *Doc. Hist. R.I.*, II, 30–31; *Winthrop Papers*, IV, 160.

exhausted the soil they moved away, and grass grew in the abandoned fields. Elsewhere the country was well forested; every kind and size of wood that the colonists would require for years to come grew there luxuriantly. In contrast with the largely unproductive lands of most of coastal Massachusetts and Plymouth Colony, here the English discovered the true bounty of Nature. The new inhabitants of the islands enjoyed the finest climate along the Atlantic seaboard, one of rapid changes within acceptable limits, which induced the greatest possible amount of human energy. Moreover, as a traveler remarked quaintly, though correctly, Newport on Rhode Island was a coat warmer in winter and a coat cooler in summer than Boston. The southerners and West Indians who went annually to Newport after 1760 in search of a restoring clime unerringly chose the right spot.[6]

Between 1636 and 1690 the population of the little colony increased to about six thousand persons, some twenty-six hundred of whom lived in Newport and its environs. To them should be added, perhaps, the three thousand more dwelling in adjoining communities belonging to New Plymouth or Massachusetts Bay. Nearly all of the families had arrived before 1660, and their natural increase doubled the population about every twenty-five years.[7]

What manner of men were these first Rhode Islanders? One does not ordinarily quote Bing Crosby as an historical authority, but years ago, upon being asked on the air who *his* ancestors were, the singer answered with the most profound and uniquely acceptable genealogical generalization this writer has ever encountered: Stock equipment, half males and half females. And so it was

6. *Winthrop's Journal*, I, 138. On the environment, see Ellsworth Huntington, *The Redman's Continent*, Chronicles of America (New Haven, 1919), chaps. 1–4, pp. 2–117; and for a more detailed treatment, see Ellsworth Huntington, *Civilization and Climate* (rev. ed., New Haven, 1924).

7. *RIHS Colls.*, X, 142n.; Richard L. Bowen, *Early Rehoboth* (Rehoboth, 1945), I, 9, 11, 17; *New England Historical and Genealogical Register*, XXXIV, 404–5.

with our Rhode Island forebears. Although most of the settlers stemmed from very humble antecedents—half males, half females —collectively they made up the purest English stock that America has ever had. These people crossed the Atlantic to New England because they wanted to; they removed a second time to Providence and Aquidneck because they had to. Almost any one of them could have begun an autobiography with the opening line Herman Melville chose for *Moby Dick* from Genesis 16:15: "Call me Ishmael."

The first Rhode Islanders were neither beginners nor bunglers, whatever their detractors may have said. For the most part husbandmen, supplemented by a few rural artisans, they had originated in the most progressive counties of England. Though few of them had had much formal education, many were able to read, and most were endowed with common sense, which restrained them from overextending themselves. From the Wampanoags and Narragansetts they quickly learned how to cultivate crops in a heavily wooded country and to make do with native foods: maize above all, peas, beans, and pumpkins; and they found in tobacco an immediately marketable staple.[8]

In their new refuge, furthermore, the firstcomers were undertaking a second round of pioneering, their first round having been experienced at the Bay Colony or at Plymouth. They knew what they wanted, and they knew how to get it. An English expert on agriculture, Dr. Robert Child, sent home to his friend Samuel Hartlib, the foremost writer on farming in England, a description of "Rhoade Ile" as early as 1645: "This place abounds with corne and cattle, especially sheep, there being nigh a 1000 on the Isle."

8. Far and away the most readable and fullest contemporary account of the Indians of New England is Roger Williams's authoritative *A Key to the Language of America: or an Help to the Language of the Natives, in that Part of America Called New England*, ed. Howard M. Chapin (Providence, 1936). It is especially apposite to this study, for it is based on the Narragansetts, the most numerous tribe in New England.

The next year, Edward Winslow of Plymouth, no friend of the exiles, said much the same thing. "Rhode Island," he observed, is "very fruitfull and plentifully abounding with all manner of food the Country affordeth, and hath two Townes, besides many great Farmes well stocked in the same."[9]

These writers are two unimpeachable witnesses to an astonishing and impressive accomplishment: the transformaticn of the wilderness bordering Narragansett Bay and also some of its larger islands into a productive rural society in a scant seven years. As Dr. Child remarked, some of the dissenters from the New England Way, called Antinomians, who found life in Boston unacceptable and left in 1637, were "banished men, yet rich." Among them were the Hutchinsons, William and Edward, William Coddington, William Brenton, John Coggeshall, John Sanford, and William Baulstone, men with mercantile and political, as well as agricultural, backgrounds in both Old and New England. Having attempted to wring ample livings out of the unyielding soil of Massachusetts over a period of eight years, they instructed their advance agent, Dr. John Clarke, who had first proposed that the Antinomians find a new place to live, to search out with the utmost care the finest and most fertile land available, land having open fields or meadows with sufficient grass for pasturing cattle or that might be mowed for hay. First he went northward to look over the Piscataqua country and, not finding what he wanted, journeyed southward overland to Providence. Advised and guided about by Roger Williams, Dr. Clarke selected a new land of Canaan on the unoccupied island of Aquidneck, with room nearby for later expansion to Hog, Prudence, Patience, Conanicut, and eventually Block islands.[10]

9. Dr. Child reported Plymouth's land as "barren" and that of Massachusetts Bay as "indifferently fruitfull." Child to Hartlib, in *CSM Pubs.*, XXXVIII, 51; Edward Winslow, *Hypocrisie Unmasked* (London, 1646), 79–80.

10. Among forty-five of the "richer inhabitants" of Boston listed in order of the size of their contributions to support "a free school master" in 1636 were: Coddington (no. 4), William Hutchinson (no. 6), Coggeshall (no. 11),

To this writer's knowledge, the significance of bay and offshore islands in the development of agriculture in southern New England has not been pointed out before. Many of these islands had some open fields or meadows, in which grass grew luxuriantly, and noble stands of timber. Nearly every parcel of land on any one of them lay close enough to the edge of the water to be readily accessible with small craft (which was definitely not true of the farm lands of interior New England); and the waters themselves teemed with large edible fish and smaller ones for fertilizing hills of corn in the fashion taught to the colonists by the aborigines.[11]

The principal advantage of the islands, however, was that they were safe lands on which to raise all kinds of livestock: first hogs, then goats, followed in time by neat cattle, sheep, and horses. Few matters take up as much space in the records of the inland towns of New England as the killing or maiming of livestock by predatory animals, wolves in particular. Here in a densely forested country, all communities were forced to offer bounties or to use other devices for cutting down the number of wolves and foxes that came out of the woods to prey upon all four-footed beasts

Harding (no. 13), William Aspinwall (no. 16), Sanford (no. 17), Cole (no. 18), Baulstone (no. 19), and Edward Hutchinson (no. 45). About the same time, Coddington, William Hutchinson, Harding, and Coggeshall (out of twelve) lent £5 each to help erect a fort at Boston. All were selectmen and prominent in the community. "Boston Records, 1634–1660," in *Second Report of the Record Commissioners* (Boston, 1902), 8, 160, *et passim;* Child to Hartlib, in *CSM Pubs.*, XXXVIII, 51; John Callender, *An Historical Discourse on the Civil and Religious Affairs of Rhode Island, RIHS Colls.*, IV, 83–84; John Clarke, *Ill Newes from New-England* (London, 1652), sig. A-3.

11. Originally Dr. Clarke wanted Sowams (Barrington), but Plymouth's jurisdiction extended to the eastern shores of the bay, and its leaders claimed "that Sow-wames was the garden of the patent, and the flower in the garden." Williams then suggested Aquidneck Island, but William Bradford notified Governor Winthrop that it was "not In our Pattente (though we tould them not so).... We thinke it is also better for us both to have some strength in that bay." Clarke, *Ill Newes from New-England*, sig. A-3; *Winthrop Papers*, IV, 23.

and small fowl. In a letter of April 1647, William Coddington explained to John Winthrop, Jr., of Fishers Island that flocks of sheep on Aquidneck doubled every year because there were no wolves on the island that were native to it. Such vermin as infested an island could be killed off easily in drives conducted by the Indian hunters customarily employed to supply the colonists with venison. This was done on Aquidneck in 1642; and the destruction of many sheep by wolves that had crossed over from the present Tiverton on the mainland led to another thorough drive of the island by the farmers of Portsmouth and Newport in 1663. Fertile, safe, easily reached by water, the islands were by far the fittest and least costly places on which to start and develop the livestock industry of southern New England.[12]

The unqualified success of agriculture on Rhode Island and some settlements on the mainland throughout the seventeenth century resulted not so much from the collective effort of many pioneer families, each toiling away on a few cleared acres to produce every year a tiny marketable surplus, as from the accomplishment of a few gentlemen who, investing large sums of money for that time and place, created in New England a species of landed estates superficially resembling those of Old England but unique in the colonies.[13]

12. Communities on the mainland suffered great damage from wolves. As late as 1680, the town meeting of Providence voted a bounty of 20s. in country pay for each wolf killed and levied a rate of £10 to support it. At least five bounties were paid within a year. *Providence Recs.*, V, 273; VIII, 80; *R.I. Col. Recs.*, I, 84, 113, 122, 124–25; *Portsmouth Recs.*, 32, 33, 52, 82–83; *Winthrop Papers*, V, 150.

13. Some colonists possessed, or knew about, contemporary books, of which the most influential were: Walter Blith, *The English Improver: or, a New Survey of Husbandry* (London, 1648); *The Book of Husbandry, by Master Fitzherbert* (London, 1634); *Samuel Hartlib His Legacie* (London, 1651); Leonard Mascall, *The Countryman's Jewel: Or the Government of Cattle* (London, 1587, and twelve more editions to 1680); Thomas Tusser, *Five Hundred Points of Good Husbandry, as well for Champion or Open*

When William Coddington and his followers left Portsmouth in 1639 to found Newport, they promptly laid out several "great Farmes." In November 1640, for instance, Captain Robert Harding, a former selectman of Boston, leased to William Withington, a carpenter of Pocasset, his Newport farm of three hundred acres consisting of meadows and woodlands, together with all appurtenances, for nine years. The tenant might cut down timber for nine years. On his part, Withington agreed that after seven years he would reassign to Harding all buildings, fences, and "draynings of medow," and also pay him a rent of £20 for each of the two years remaining under the lease. He was also to keep all draining ditches and structures in repair for seven years. By the agreement, also, Harding turned over eight cows with calf and a young bull (worth ten cows), and two sows, which Withington was to repay after nine years with ten cows and ten of the increase. The former carpenter's herd had grown sufficiently by 1649 to enable him to repay Captain Harding and to ship to Barbados twelve cattle and a ton of corn to feed them—all of which seems to justify his assumption of the title of merchant.[14]

A second tract of 300 acres was granted by the Town of Newport

---

Country as for Woodland or Several (London, 1557, and seventeen editions to 1638); John Worlidge, *Systema Agricultura, Being the Mystery of Husbandry Discovered and layd Open by J. W.* (London, 1669). The copy of the last named (probably the best work available), which is in the Winthrop MSS in the MHS, was presented by Samuel Hartlib to John Winthrop, Jr. There were four editions to 1689, and the Library Company of Philadelphia has them all.

For English farming, the most recent useful works are: Joan Thirsk, ed., *The Agrarian History of England and Wales, 1500–1640* (Cambridge, England, 1967), IV; William E. Minchinton, ed., *Essays in Agrarian History* (New York, 1968), I; Robert Trow-Smith, *A History of British Live-Stock Husbandry to 1700* (London, 1957), and *Life From the Land: The Growth of Farming in Western Europe* (London, 1967).

14. At the end of nine years, Harding was also to buy all carts, wains, and "husbandry instruments" on the farm. *Note-Book kept by Thomas Lechford Esq. . . . , Archaeologia Americana*, VII (Cambridge, 1885), 330–33.

to Robert Harding in 1641. Five years later when he deeded it to David Selleck of Boston, soapboiler, Richard Carder and Edward Thurston were his joint tenants. With the land went all houses, out-buildings, and livestock (four oxen, two cows, two heifers, twelve goats, and a ram), and various farm implements, including a plow, two coulters, and twenty-five harrow teeth. In 1668, the two parcels (estimated at 574 acres and by this time called Hammersmith Farm), the mansions, farm buildings, barns, and outhouses became the property of William Brenton.[15]

An even more spectacular farming enterprise was that of William Coddington. Whatever odium has attached to his political ter-giversations, he was, until his death in 1678, the foremost stockman —agriculturalist in fact—in all New England. In his case, as well as those of Captain Harding and others, the husbandry was limited almost exclusively to stock raising and grazing. It is striking that these holders of large estates succeeded in finding some colonists who were willing to become tenants in a region where land for small farms might be had for nothing or for a very small cost. Jer-emy Gould covenanted in 1642 to maintain himself, his wife, a maidservant, and "5 able men, kind, good workers, to bee imployed upon and about" the 350-acre farm of William Coddington, "Gent.," and to keep the owner's sixty female goats and three "sheep rams" for three years for half of the increase and all of the milk during that time. In the same agreement, Coddington devised eight cows to be kept for a five-year period in return for half of the increase. Gould also promised to improve the land on the farm; and in four years he had broken up one hundred acres on which he was growing fifteen hundred bushels of Indian corn annually. He also, by this same year, had raised twelve oxen, a stone-horse, and a mare.[16]

Coddington, far from satisfied with Gould's performance and attitude, complained that his tenant had not employed himself

15. R.I. Land Evidences, I, 344–47, 431–34.
16. R.I. Land Evidences, I, 62–j; *Doc. Hist. R.I.*, II, 158–60, 162–64.

and "those other eight persons before Covenanted to the best of the demised premises"; rather he had obviously employed the oxen and horse for his own use and profit on the fields he had cleared. Nor, in the landlord's opinion, had Gould kept the fences sufficiently mended for the "safety of the corn and seed sowen" from intrusions of livestock; furthermore he had not exerted the "best of his skill for the manuring of the demised premises in keeping it fitt for tillage" but had instead "worne itt out for want of good manuring." Listing numerous other breaches of the covenant, Coddington presented a claim of over £1,000 against Gould. Perhaps the fact that two years before this, on a farm that he operated himself, William Coddington had suffered an estimated loss of from £400 to £500 sterling when a nighttime fire consumed a "large Corne Barne" worth £150 with all of his seed corn, twelve oxen, eight cows, six other beasts, his farmhouse, bedding, and all of his "household stuff" made the losses on his leased farm the more worrisome (plate 1). Tenancy clearly did not always prove to be satisfactory, but it did serve to lessen the shortage of farm labor and to speed the clearing and breaking-up of virgin land.[17]

All over the colony, side by side with the great estates of Portsmouth and Newport, could be seen many small farms ranging from four to sixty acres. The Proprietors Records of Newport show that in 1639, 1641, and 1644 land was laid out in grants to individual inhabitants; what was left was retained in common for the proprietors. Additionally, each servant who had come with the first settlers received a parcel of land at the expiration of his term: William Coddington's man John Fairfield had ten acres confirmed to him in 1653, as did another servant, Robert Taylor, two years later. With the passage of time, some of the more enterprising and successful of the small holders followed the example of the

17. "Manuring" meant cultivating, hoeing, etc., as much as it did its modern sense. See *Oxford English Dictionary*, s.v. "manure"; R.I. Land Evidences, I, 6b–e, g–h; *Winthrop Papers*, IV, 489–90.

great landowners and bought up other men's property to con-
solidate with their own farms, while others made large profits by
selling off improved acreages. No inhabitant of Portsmouth turned
out to be more acquisitive than Thomas Lawton, who had started
out in a very modest way.[18]

The small farmers of Providence, Pawtuxet, and Warwick ex-
perienced very little competition from the owners of large estates.
Throughout the entire colony, these yeomen grew Indian corn
and hay, planted apple orchards in order to make cider, and
raised swine for the pork. On farms of a middling size, some of
them produced a small surplus each year for sale to outsiders.
Although at Cocumscussoc in 1679 Richard Smith recorded "a
great yeare for frute and Coren; Sider in abundans," it was not
until well after the end of King Philip's War (1676) that the
farmers of Providence, Pawtuxet, and Warwick fully recovered
from the burning of barns and houses and the driving away of
their livestock by the Narragansetts. Ten years after the conflict,
however, Edward Randolph, writing to England about a grant
of a thousand acres at Warwick, alleged "R. Island to be the best
land and for that quantity the most profitable part of New Eng-
land." Not before 1690 did more than a handful of energetic and
venturesome men from Aquidneck move westward across the bay
to begin the first settlement in the Narragansett Country.[19]

The migration of Anne Hutchinson and her followers to Rhode
Island was much more than a flight from religious persecution. It

18. See Appendix I for landholding at Newport. Records of the Island of
Rhode Island (MS, R.I. Archives), 11; Horace E. Turner, comp., Colonial
Land Evidences (MS, NHS); Proprietors' Records, Newport (MS, New
York Public Library), Misc. Box, R.I.; R.I. Land Evidences, I, 15–16, 19–29,
125–26. For the disposition of land at Portsmouth, see *Portsmouth Recs.*, 32.

19. *Portsmouth Recs.*, 298, 301, 311, 316; R.I. Land Evidences, I, 10;
RIHS Colls., X, 277; R. N. Toppan and A. T. S. Goodrick, eds., *Edward
Randolph . . .*, Prince Society Publications (Boston, 1909), VI, 179.

was an agricultural-commercial experiment that had been thoughtfully and minutely planned in advance at Boston and adequately financed by men who were thoroughly familiar with the management of estates. As sometime merchants, they realized fully that the new rural communities they intended to establish would, like all colonial ventures, have to be supplied from the outset with manufactured goods and other necessary commodities from overseas. To purchase these they had to produce some kind or kinds of returns promptly or their new colony would fail.[20]

Wholly overlooked by posterity has been the extraordinary wisdom exhibited by these migrants, who perceived that the economic activities of the new society they were founding must be fitted into the grand design of the long-established agricultural-commercial system of England, the nature of which was just being elucidated by Thomas Mun and other writers about winning treasure by foreign trade. The planners at Boston were acutely aware that they had to keep steadily in mind two major considerations: the connection of their colony with the outside world and the creation of the kind of rural economy that would produce merchantable commodities quickly in a land whose towering forests presented a dismaying obstacle to any repetition of the familiar tillage of Britain. Their solution was to undertake a different kind of farming from that practiced in Massachusetts by entering into agriculture on both large and small farms and, at the same time, to foster commerce of a suitable kind with their neighbors as quickly as possible.[21]

What the Rhode Islanders accomplished can best be realized by examining the maritime scene up to 1657, when the coming of the Quakers gave the impetus for an important leap forward by the commerce of Narragansett Bay. Though preferring English meth-

20. The planning at Boston can be deduced from Coddington's letters in the *Winthrop Papers* and other materials of his.

21. A superb work on the Mother Country at this time is Charles Wilson's *England's Apprenticeship* (London, 1965).

ods of business and English manufactures and enjoying the friendship of and credit from Boston merchants, the settlers nevertheless resented and mistrusted the motives of the authorities of the Massachusetts port. Consequently they tended to traffic to the southwest rather than to the northeast, encouraged thereto not only by the Dutch of Manhattan but by the protected waterway of Long Island Sound.

At Newport on September 19, 1642, the General Court of Rhode Island directed that "the Governour and Deputie shall treat with the Governour of the Dutch to supply us with necessities, and to take of our commodities at such rates as may be suitable." This meant that William Coddington and William Brenton, both one-time merchants, had concluded that the new colony had advanced economically to the point where formal action ought to be taken to promote trade. Throughout the forties, most of the growing carrying trade between New Netherland and Rhode Island went on in Dutch bottoms. Skippers Arent Isaac, Cornelis Melyn, and Captain John Underhill frequented both Newport and the post of Richard Smith at Cocumscussoc. And despite the ban on all Dutch traffic with the Indians of Rhode Island during the first Dutch War (1652–54), John Garious (Garriad, Gariardy, Gerard), possibly a Fleming, who married the sister of John Warner of Warwick, traded for furs with Ezekiel Holliman and John Greene, Jr., on the west shore of the bay. A few Rhode Islanders, notably John Throgmorton (whose name is perpetuated at Throgs Neck in Westchester County), made voyages to Manhattan in their shallops with some regularity. Relations with the Dutch inevitably drew vessels from Narragansett Bay into commercial exchanges at New London, New Haven, and Fairfield in Connecticut, as well as the towns of Long Island from Southampton on the Atlantic and along the sound to Oyster Bay.[22]

Newport was properly named, for the little town gave evidence

22. Records of the Island of Rhode Island, 64; *RIHS Colls.*, XXVIII, 72–73, 75; R.I. Land Evidences, I, 2, 149–51; *R.I. Col. Recs.*, I, 126, 243, 274;

of steadily increasing shipping activity after 1640. In August of that
year, Mathew Sutherland and Thomas Robinson, mariners, were
given a shallop of 4 tons burthen with a mainsail, compass, oars,
and anchor cable, "all new," by the agent of the Earl of Stirling,
James Forret of Long Island, in part payment of a debt he owed
them. Actions for debt and failure to perform services on the part
of mariners and merchants of Boston and Newport were not at
all infrequent. Numerous ship's protests appear in the records,
and the first Assembly under the Warwick Patent held at Ports-
mouth May 19–21, 1647, adopted "the Sea Lawes, otherwise called
the Laws of Oleron," for "the benefit of Seamen (upon the Island)."
At this same time, provision was made for a provincial seal con-
sisting of the motto HOPE and a shield with a fouled anchor
signifying recognition of the maritime nature of the community.
The Assembly further agreed upon setting reciprocal duties with
foreign nations on all goods exchanged, except beaver pelts, and
forbade all foreigners to chaffer with the natives.[23]

A series of events in the year 1649 testified dramatically to the
importance of shipping to the infant colony. The Town Meeting
of Portsmouth deemed it necessary to appoint Thomas Gorton as
its first water bailiff. The former carpenter turned merchant,
William Withington, apparently inaugurated the West Indies and
the slave traffics on June 11 when he hired from Henry Parkes
half of the ship *Beginning*, 40 tons, to accommodate twelve Rhode

Narragansett Historical Register, VIII, 265–66; *MHS Colls.*, 4th ser., VI,
284–85; *Winthrop Papers*, IV, 248; V, 283, 287, 326.

23. Too much reliance has been placed hitherto on Callender's statement
about Newport: "The trade and business of the town at the first, was but very
little and inconsiderable, consisting only of a little corn, and pork and tobacco,
sent to Boston for a few European and other goods they could not subsist
without, and all at the mercy of the traders there too." *Historical Discourse*,
95; Lechford, *Note-Book*, 283, 301; *R.I. Col. Recs.*, I, 151; *Doc. Hist. R.I.*,
II, 135, 149, 153.

Island cattle and the necessary hay and corn for a voyage to Barbados and "Guinney" and return by way of Barbados, Antigua, and Boston. Men in a "loyter," who boarded a ship arriving in Narragansett Bay from England, were the first to learn of the execution of King Charles I, "but no particulars," news which elicited an excited letter from Roger Williams to John Winthrop, Jr. Two months after this, "Captain Jeremiah [Jeremy] Clarke of Road Island" became the principal owner of "the good barque called the Sea flowre," which, as far as the scanty records reveal, may have been the first locally owned vessel larger than a shallop to sail out of Newport. Finally, in November, one Captain Blaufeld, a Dutch privateer, conferred upon Newport the questionable honor of making it his base for disposing of prizes. "Flushed with blood" and intending a voyage to the West Indies, some of the Frenchmen belonging to the privateer purchased a frigate from Captain Jeremy Clarke.[24]

At no time, however, did the Rhode Islanders sever their connection with Boston or allow it to lapse. John Throgmorton from Salem had been one of the first arrivals at Providence in 1636, and he kept a shallop constantly in service, making trips to the Bay Town and, occasionally, to Salem with cargoes of wheat from Long Island and Connecticut, and pork and corn from Narragansett Bay. With the founding of Pequot, or New London, by John Winthrop, Jr., in 1647 and the settling of Fishers and Shelter islands and several towns on eastern Long Island, vessels from the Bay Colony rounded Cape Cod with increasing frequency; and ordinarily they touched at Newport. William Withington and other Newport merchants procured English linens and woolens, hardware, iron, and other goods by way of Boston, where, too, they could buy bills of exchange with island-grown tobacco with which to pay

24. *Portsmouth Recs.*, 42, 50; *Aspinwall Recs.*, 121, 220, 233–34, 265; "Letters of Roger Williams," in *Narr. Club Pubs.*, VI, 196; *Winthrop Papers*, V, 353, 376.

for their imports. And for their part, the Massachusetts Bay traders discreetly sublimated religious prejudices as long as they could turn an honest shilling by such dealings.[25]

Commercial relations with Massachusetts Bay increased noticeably early in the fifties, especially when the first Dutch War cut off trade with Manhattan, and the traffic continued after it ended. In August 1651, for example, David Selleck and Peter Gardner of Roxbury came to Narragansett Bay to fetch the corn of Roger Williams and of Stephen Paine of Seekonk: "They are bound to the French," Williams wrote to John Winthrop, Jr. By 1655 Christopher Almy (formerly of Scituate), William Dyer, and several inhabitants of Aquidneck had acquired small vessels fit for coasting voyages, and in November of this year, Roger Williams found it necessary to remind the General Court of Massachusetts Bay: "(I humbly conceive), with the people of this colony your commerce is as great as with any in the country"—including Connecticut, apparently.[26]

Thus it came about that by the year 1657 the Colony of Rhode Island and Providence Plantations was producing annually enough of an agricultural surplus to attract traders from New Amsterdam, Salem, and Boston; and further, that the inhabitants had begun to export some of it in their own vessels. Small by modern standards as this surplus and the shipping which carried it away were, for the New England of the day they were both substantial and important. Shortly traffic would mount.

25. *Winthrop Papers*, V, 288–89; *MHS Procs.*, XIV, 271; *Aspinwall Recs.*, 121, 220, 322, 388, 411, 412.

26. John Throgmorton traded at Providence and Warwick, and in 1639 he rented, for three years, Prudence Island, where he built a wharf. John O. Austin, *Genealogical Dictionary of Rhode Island* (Albany, 1887), 200; *Narr. Club Pubs.*, VI, 212–13; *R.I. Col. Recs.*, I, 324.

III

THE DENIZENS

OF NABOTH'S MEADOWS

THE first settlers—rich, middling, and poor—who located themselves on Aquidneck and adjacent islands of Narragansett Bay passed through the subsistence-farming phase so quickly that it might be said that they beat the frontier; and by 1641 they were already establishing a rural society characterized by a commercial agriculture. From the very outset they prospered. We have seen that this was no accident, no simple, hit-or-miss accomplishment but rather a very complex combination of able leadership, vision, daring, ample capital, hard work, and (not to be underestimated) a generous measure of chance.

Those men, whom the age denominated adventurers, such as Coddington, Brenton, Coggeshall, Harding, and possibly one or two more, had worked out in advance of settlement a form of "agricultural adaptation" that differed noticeably from contemporary English farming. Assured of ample tracts of fertile land—with more easily available when they wanted them—these merchant-experimenters utilized the whole ecological scene for their own purposes and profit. They avoided the rigid conservatism of the small farmer and shifted from intensive mixed tillage emphasizing wheat to an extensive pastoral husbandry. From the aborigines they borrowed methods and plants freely; they exploited safe pastures on the islands; they made the several wooden by-products of forest clearing yield them profitable cargoes. But the real secret of their success was grazing, breeding, and fattening of livestock to vend in distant markets and the growing of only such selected grains as they required for their own provisions and the feeding of their beasts.

A system of agriculture soon emerged that bore very little resemblance to the mixed grain and animal industry of Britain. The men of Aquidneck led the way in this remarkable development, which elicited highly favorable comments from observers of the caliber of Dr. Robert Child, Samuel Maverick, and John Josselyn. By 1660 farmers at Providence and, after 1676, of the Narragansett Country were adopting their methods. The Rhode Island way of husbandry spread into neighboring parts of Plymouth Colony, was widely imitated in eastern Connecticut and up the valley of its great river, even across the sound on Long Island, and up the Merrimack Valley of Massachusetts Bay.

The open spaces on Aquidneck, already cleared by the Wampanoags, were immediately occupied and planted in 1638–39, but further clearing by "gurdling" trees and allowing them to die, or by chopping them down, soon became necessary. Rich landowners leased parcels of land to tenants to clear and break up, while some of the small farmers depended on one or two indentured servants to assist the members of the family in this arduous work. The experience that the average colonist had acquired during a stay of from one to eight years in the Bay Colony in the clearing and breaking up of land doubtless stood him in better stead than any other rural activity.[1]

The few natives who were cultivating fields when the colonists arrived kindly showed them, if they were not already familiar with their customs, their multicrop method of planting four seeds of Indian corn, or maize, to a hill along with peas, beans, and

1. Rhode Islanders apparently did not consider it necessary to "stubb all Staddle" (grub out all small trees) or to roll their planted barley with a large wooden roller to break up the clods as did the first settlers of Connecticut and New Haven. Jared Eliot, *Essays on Field Husbandry*, ed. Harry J. Carman and Rexford G. Tugwell (New York, 1934), 7, 40.

pumpkins. All preparing of the soil necessary for cultivating could be done with a hoe so that there was no need for the settlers to have "staddled" and plowed fields for these crops; moreover, the English methods were labor-consuming. And labor was at a premium. Nor was there any need to prepare land in the English fashion before they set out great numbers of apple trees whose fruits were pressed into an excellent cider, which was more widely consumed than beer and often exported. In about a decade, however, crops requiring well-cleared and well-plowed fields were being grown: barley to malt for beer, rye for winter feed for sheep, oats for the horses, wheat in small quantities for local domestic use, and flax for making linen thread. Of East Anglia before 1622, Michael Drayton had sung in *Poly-Olbion* about "the turnip tasting well to clownes in winter weather." Some farmers of Portsmouth grew turnips (probably as food for themselves rather than to revive the soil). But throughout the colony, as well as on Rhode Island, Indian corn was still the principal grain raised.[2]

Like the natives, the English settlers made corn their staple food, which they prepared in several forms, one of which was the now-celebrated Rhode Island jonnycake; unlike the Indians, they also fed corn to their animals. As the demand for it mounted, they found a way to increase the yield by plowing single furrows about six feet apart and then cross-plowing at the same distance. Where the furrows intersected, the husbandman planted his seeds, which he covered by hoeing or plowing another furrow close by. Of Rhode Island in 1645, Dr. Child could assert that "this place abounds with corne," and it continued throughout the century to

2. By his will in 1671, Richard Borden of Portsmouth left to his widow the "use of thirty fruit trees in his orchard." John O. Austin, *Genealogical Dictionary of Rhode Island* (Albany, 1887), 23; *Portsmouth Recs.*, 390, 402; Suffolk County, Mass., Probate Records (MSS, Court House, Boston), VII, 39–40, 43; Douglass E. Leach, *A Rhode Islander Reports on King Philip's War: The Second William Harris Letter of August, 1676* (Providence, 1963), 47.

be the leading crop. John Winthrop, Jr., attributed this increase—which he thought had doubled by 1662—to fertilizing: putting one to three "Alooses," or alewives, in each hill. "The English have learned this good husbandry of the Indians and do still use it in places," also moose manure and, near fishing stages, heads and guts, "the Garbage of Codfish." By this time many farmers were turning to rotted cow dung as a fertilizer, readily available by reason of the many cattle on Rhode Island. In 1664 the Royal Commissioners reported that seeds of corn planted on Rhode Island yielded eighty for one and that some farmers had grown it for twenty-six years "without manuring." Shelled corn provided Rhode Islanders with their first export crop, and in time local water mills, or windmills, ground many bushels of meal for the Boston and Caribbean markets. In truth, among other crops of the Narragansett region, only peas were ever produced in quantities large enough to make a commercial staple; and only oats ever ranked with corn and peas as commodities acceptable at stated rates for provincial taxes.[3]

For approximately ten years after 1641, William Coddington and one or two other large landholders experimented with tobacco because of its market value, but it never was a successful crop. Peter Gardner of Roxbury shipped from Boston in the *Supply* for London in October 1649 four butts, eight hogsheads, and one barrel of "tobacco which grew at Roade Iland as Mr. Coddington and Mr. Baulston do certify under theire hands." Mr. William Alford of Boston "laded aboard the shipp *Trades Increase* . . . three barrells of Tobacco marked W and all the Tobacco was

3. Throughout the period 1638–90, wheat was imported at Newport from Connecticut and Long Island in coasters for the baking of ship's bread or biscuit (hardtack) for use on shipboard. William and Thomas Richardson, Account Book, 1662–1702 (MS, NHS), 4; Fulmer Mood, "John Winthrop, Jr., on Indian Corn," in *NEQ*, X, 121–32; Child to Hartlib, in *CSM Pubs.*, XXXVIII, 51; Lewes Roberts, *Merchants Mappe of Commerce* (London, 1671), 53–54; Stevens, Transcripts, I, no. 66; *R.I. Col. Recs.*, II, 78.

planted at Road Island." In that same month in 1650, Peter Gardner shipped "two butts, one puncheon, one dry fatt and seven hogs-heades of Tobacco planted at Roade Island as two of theire magistrates testify. The mark is P. G." When the *Providence*, Ralph Parker master, sailed for Newfoundland in 1652, Christopher Almy of Portsmouth, a coaster, shipped fifty-nine rolls of tobacco plus some flour and peas, which he almost certainly exchanged for Dutch brandy. Though the weed became increasingly important in Rhode Island cargoes after 1660, it was procured from the southward, and nothing is recorded of local tobacco culture after this date.[4]

Plenty of good grass fit for making hay was essential to the prospective grazier for feeding his cattle in the winter and pasturing them in the summer. The hay of the salt marshes and open meadows, which grew so luxuriantly, attracted the attention of Dr. John Clarke and his party in 1638. In August of that year the inhabitants of Portsmouth granted "the Remainder of the Grass, which is yett uncut at hogg Island" to the newest freeman, William Brenton, that he might "mowe this yeare for his necessity." The next year, when Newport was named, its limits on Rhode Island, "together with the small Ilands and the grass of Connunegott [Conanicut] . . . appointed for the accommodation of the . . . Towne," were defined. Within Newport itself all the meadowlands were soon laid out at the rate of three hundred acres of upland for every twenty cows. The Rhode Island authorities in 1640 ordered the governor to write to Plymouth Colony "about their Title of the Maine Land Grass" across the Sakonnet River in the present town of Tiverton. But, alas for all the planning, the native grass turned out to lack sufficient nutrition for beasts—in fact, no variety of grass in eastern North America had much food value.[5]

The most spectacular aspect of "improving the wildernesse" of the Colony of Rhode Island and Providence Plantations was the

4. *Aspinwall Recs.*, 411, 412; *Providence Recs.*, XV, 51, 55.
5. *Doc. Hist. R.I.*, II, 43; *R.I. Col. Recs.*, I, 88, 96, 103.

introduction of English grass. Almost in desperation, Rhode Island farmers began to sow varieties of English hay and grass seed, for the very existence of the new plantation hinged upon nutritious grass. We can reasonably assume that the great landowners who had the money, William Coddington in particular, procured the seed from overseas and distributed it not only on Aquidneck but to the small farmers about Providence. When John Winthrop, Jr., was setting up his great plantation on Fishers Island in 1647, Robert Williams, at his brother Roger's solicitation, shipped to Winthrop twelve bushels of five sorts of English hayseed, which he had "heaped for allowance." Captain John Throgmorton, whose vessel was carrying the seed to Fishers Island, Williams advised, was reputed to have "much experience how you shall order the same," which is suited both for "moowing and feeding of Cattell." Williams charged 5s. a bushel for the seed at Providence; the freight was additional. On May 24 of this same year, John Coggeshall, unsolicited, sent another twelve bushels to Winthrop: "I filled the sakes, because I know you will not repent it, and also I want corne." Coggeshall sold his seed at Newport for 5s. a bushel.[6]

It seems that the otherwise well informed John Winthrop, Jr., knew very little about the sowing of hayseed and asked for directions. Coggeshall sent him some good instructions on May 24, but the observations that Roger Williams collected from his brother and neighbors and dispatched five days later were more detailed and give a very good idea of how the colonists grew grass and hay:

First usually 3 bushells seeds to one Acre land.
2. It hath bene knowne to spread to mat etc. the Indian hills being only scrapt or leveld.
3. This may be done at any time of the yeare (but the sooner the better).
4. It is best to sow upon a rayne preceding.

6. *Winthrop Papers*, V, 148–49, 165–66.

5. Some say let the ripe grasse stand untill it seede and the wind disperse it (susque deque) up and downe for it is of that thriving and homogeneall nature with the earth that the very dung of Cattell that feeds on it will produce the grass.

6. The offs which can hardly be severed from the seeds hath the same productive facultie.

7. Sow it not in an Orchard neere fruit trees for it will steale and rob the Trees etc.[7]

That Coggeshall, Robert Williams, and "other neighbours" of Newport and Providence could act as seed merchants (as well as growers) and sell such quantities at 5s. a bushel reveals that hayseed was already home-grown and widely sown in the fields around these towns. In 1664 the Royal Commissioners emphasized that the best English grass grew in the colony, and more than a decade later the Reverend William Hubbard mentioned in *A General History of New England* that on Rhode Island grass "doth much abound, more than [in] the rest of the country."[8]

Two further undertakings were essential to "improving the wildernesse," as the settlers referred to the preparation of ground either for tillage or grazing. One of these was the draining of meadows, swamps, and marshes where salt hay grew. To men raised in Cambridgeshire or the Fen Country, digging with trenching tools was not unfamiliar, though in their new home not as much digging was called for, especially on the high ground of Rhode Island, as in eastern England.[9]

7. *Winthrop Papers*, V, 166, 168.

8. Stevens, Transcripts, I, no. 66; William Hubbard, *A General History of New England from the Discovery to MDCLXXX* (Cambridge, 1815), 345.

9. Dr. Joan Thirsk reminds us that in Britain "in the sixteenth and early seventeenth centuries men made war upon the forests, moors, and fens with a zeal they had not felt for some three hundred years. They cleared woods and drained wet low-lying land to make new pastures, they turned old

Far more pressing was the need for fencing to keep the livestock of a pastoral economy from breaking into, trampling, and consuming the crops in cornfields and hayfields. In December 1639, a Quarter Court ordered that "ther shall be sufficient fences, eyther hedge or post and raile, made about the Corne Grounds that shall be planted or sowne" on Rhode Island, and set a forfeit of 3s. 4d. for every rod of fencing found defective. The extent of the enclosures needed on Rhode Island alone is of real significance. At Newport in 1654, William Dyer's house, yard, and two adjoining fields were "fenced in with pallisadoes and poles [posts and rails] containing 20 or 30 akers more or lesse sowed with English grasse." The town of Portsmouth voted in 1663 that "all out fences" that were four and one-half feet high should be judged sufficient, provided that the space between each rail did not exceed four inches and the fence was "sufishently Staked and pould." At Providence in 1683 Richard Bailey made thirty posts and two hundred "hewed rails" for which he charged Thomas Ward of Newport 42s. This price suggests a scarcity of timber for fencing at Aquidneck.[10]

As time passed the ever-larger amounts of timber needed for post-and-rail fences made such improvements costly. Labor charges for constructing fences mounted also. On the other hand, protection against the ravages of large herds of cattle and flocks of sheep became a necessity. The Town Meeting of Portsmouth in 1671 moved to reduce "the many Damages done in Corne and Grass, and many Catle hurt and many hart burneings amongst Neighbours" by ordering that farmers who erected "a fence Called a

---

pastures into cornland, old cornland into grass." Joan Thirsk, ed., *The Agrarian History of England and Wales, 1500–1640* (Cambridge, England, 1967), IV, 2.

10. John Hall sued William England at Portsmouth in 1644 for the return of "14 score of railes" he had carried off. *Doc. Hist. R.I.*, II, 151; *R.I. Col. Recs.*, I, 96; R.I. Land Evidences, I, 107a; RIHS, MSS, I, 37; *Portsmouth Recs.*, 117.

Virginia [snake] fence" must build it four and one-half feet high according to specifications, and post-and-rail fences should also be of that height. In addition the inhabitants voted instructions for the proper planting of hedges or for a "hedg and Ditch." Four viewers were appointed to inspect fences for any deficiencies or failures. Not until 1651 do we find any mention of the most familiar and pleasing of Rhode Island fences, when Ralph Earle and John Tripp of Portsmouth agreed in writing to make respectively forty and twenty rods of "stone wall" to fence off their cattle. Three decades passed before another Portsmouth farmer, George Sisson, was paid in land by John Cooke for "the makeing of forty seven Rods of good Suffitient Stone wall." Fencing of any sort called for a large expenditure of precious labor, but these enclosures were among the most necessary improvements on a Rhode Island farm, and usually received specific mention in land transfers. Indeed, they ranked high in public concern.[11]

The brief stay of Peter Folger, "late of Martin's Vinyard" but most recently of Newport, as a tenant farmer at Portsmouth in 1662 epitomizes the whole time-consuming and laborious process of clearing and breaking Rhode Island land for proper grazing. On October 8, the grandfather of Benjamin Franklin "hiered" from William Corey his "now dweling House and all the land that is now fenced on both sides" for five years. For the "Rent" Folger contracted to clear two acres of swamp in each of the five years: "to Cut it out and lay it [timber and brush] on heaps," and also to sow three pounds of "Clear hay-seed" upon every two acres,

11. Daniel Gookin described the Narragansett and Warwick tribes in 1674: ". . . they are an active laborious, and ingenious people, which is demonstrated in their labours they do for the English of whom more are employed, especially in *making stone fences*, and many other hard labours, than any other Indian people or neighbors." *MHS Colls.*, I, 210 (italics mine); *Portsmouth Recs.*, 53–55, 160–61, 237–39; *R.I. Land Evidences*, I, 169; RIHS, MSS, I, 12.

and "to Rive out two hundred and a half Rayles" by the next spring on the far side of the swamp to pay for the rails already put in the lower fence by Corey. As far as his strength permitted, Peter Folger might improve the land for the contracted period but he could not cut any timber on the unbroken upland unless it was needed to repair or make new fences. Moreover, it was stipulated that all trees fourteen inches thick and over at a foot above the ground could "only be gurdled and not fald." Not until December 3 did the selectmen of Portsmouth decide to let him be a resident for the term of his lease. In the fall of 1664, overwhelmed by his obligations and probably thinking, if not actually muttering to himself, "swamp-clearing be damned," the former weaver and schoolmaster quitted both farming and Rhode Island for Nantucket and the less arduous career of a miller and public official. Thereafter the Folgers and Franklins understandably clung to town life and the handicrafts.[12]

All the while that the founders of the Rhode Island colony were industriously making the land fit for husbandry, they had simultaneously to solve many problems of day-to-day living. Above everything else, there was the immediate matter of shelter. The Hutchinsons and their followers spent the winter of 1638 in caves or hovels thrown together in haste and intended only to afford temporary protection from the elements. Roofed with thatch, the first structures must have resembled the "cottage" on the east bank of the Pawcatuck River that Madam Sarah Knight described in 1704: "This little Hutt . . . was suported with shores enclosed with Clapbords, laid on Lengthways, and so much asunder, that the Light come throu' every where; the doore tyed on with a cord in the place of hinges; The floor the bear earth, no windows but such as the thin covering afforded, not any furniture but a Bedd with a glass Bottle hanging at the head on't; an earthan cupp, a small pewter Bason, A Bord with sticks to stand on, instead of a table, and a block or two in the corner instead of chairs."[13]

12. *Portsmouth Recs.*, 113, 395–96.
13. Thomas Hutchinson, *History of the Colony and Province of Massa-*

Quickly, however, the Rhode Islanders set about building permanent, or semipermanent, dwelling houses. Because all of these structures disappeared long ago, their nature can only be conjectured by piecing together scattered items found in deeds, wills, and inventories. It is safe, surely, to describe them as one-room or two-room structures, scantily furnished, and though there were some with shingled roofs, the great majority had thatched ones. As time passed and a family grew larger, or more prosperous, the first crude house was added to or replaced. During King Philip's War (1675-76) nearly all of the farmhouses in the colony, except those on Aquidneck and Conanicut, were burned. In the rebuilding (1676-90) most of the chimneys constructed were of stone, for the ravaged province contained the only limestone yet discovered in all of New England. Nevertheless the cautious comment of Governor Peleg Sanford in his report to the Lords of Trade in 1680 was essentially accurate: "The generality of our buildings is of Timber and generally small." The story-and-a-half house erected by Thomas Clemence up the valley of the Woonasquatucket River in what is now Johnston is a faithful restoration of a type of farmhouse unique to Rhode Island Colony—"a stone-ender." (See plate 3.) [14]
Several of the most substantial men of Rhode Island undertook to erect "mansion houses," which, according to the usage of the age, meant solid, separate buildings, but not "great houses." They

---

chusetts-Bay, ed. Lawrence S. Mayo (Cambridge, 1936), I, 64n.; The Journal of Madam Knight, ed. George P. Winship (facsimile of ed. of 1920, New York, 1935), 23-24.

14. In the period 1649-55, some settlers were enlarging their first permanent houses. At Warwick, for example, John Cooke deeded to Henry Knoles from Portsmouth in 1655 "my dwelling house and Lott with the outhouses" and also "the sawen Timber and Clapboards which I have provided towards another Roome." R.I. Land Evidences, I, 233-35; Austin, Genealogical Dictionary, 23; New England Historical and Genealogical Register, V, 248-49; Providence Recs., VIII, 115-16; New York Times, June 15, 1947; John H. Cady, "Thomas Clemence House," in Old-Time New England, XXXIX, 17-22; XLIII, 29; Stevens, Transcripts, II, no. 153.

were, however, carefully mentioned in all wills and deeds separately from the "dwelling houses" of ordinary farmers. The best known of the early mansions are those of William Coddington (1641) and Henry Bull (1640) at Newport. Bull also had a good house at Portsmouth in 1643, for he went to court to prevent Ralph Earle, carpenter, from removing anything from the premises that was "nayld or pinned." The construction of an "English House" called for the aid of "sufficient workmen," such as John West, whom John Richman employed to build his mansion by the mill brook at Newport in 1646. William Carpenter, a housewright of Amesbury in Massachusetts Bay, was brought down to Providence to build a mansion for William Harris, who advised London officials in 1675 that "in Rhode Island the Houses are very good, especially at a Town called Newport."[15]

In a well-wooded country, timber felled in clearing the land could be put to many uses. On Rhode Island from 1638 to 1660 and again from 1676 to 1680, most of it went into the construction of houses, barns, and other farm structures. Barns came second only to dwellings and were often built on the largest estates concurrently with mansions. William Coddington had a "larg Corne Barne" in which he also housed twelve oxen, eight cows, and some other animals during the wintertime. Having been a shepherd at one time, George Fox recognized these buildings as "great barns" because they were framed larger than those of Lincolnshire, Essex, or Devon, where one never used the term *cow barn*. (See plate 1.) During a visit to Rhode Island in 1672, Fox preached at

15. Walter Todd of Warwick deeded to Ralph Cowland of Newport in 1649 a "mansion house and a Lot" of three acres at Portsmouth, also "all old hovils," outhouses, and "fences standing." R.I. Land Evidences, I, 6f–g, 40; *Doc. Hist. R.I.*, pls. facing pp. 44, 64, 140; Antoinette Downing and Vincent Scully, Jr., *The Architectural Heritage of Newport, 1640–1915* (Cambridge, 1952), pls. 23–25, 27; William B. Weeden, *Early Rhode Island* (New York, 1910), 87; *RIHS Colls.*, X, 144.

Providence in "a great barn . . . full of people," and in a "justice's barn" at Narragansett. On most farms there was a barnyard, around which clustered a variety of small outbuildings and "appurtenances," such as sheds, dairies, and other structures used for weaving or special purposes generally related to the livestock industry.[16]

EXPERIENCED English agriculturalists had known for nearly a century that grazing required far less work than the cultivation of grain, and that certain kinds of land not suited to intensive tillage proved to be satisfactory for pasturing. The colonists had learned in the New World that it took less labor to grow Indian corn than other crops. In shipping weights, furthermore, a pound of meat or a pound of wool was worth more by far than a pound of wheat; and livestock could move to markets on the hoof in droves. In addition to these advantages, stock farming offered the signal one that it necessitated far less expenditure of labor and substance for clearing and preparing the land.[17]

For these reasons all of the planning of the rich planters at Boston before they departed in 1638 and all of their activity in clearing land, erecting buildings, and planting corn and hay after they reached the new Canaan were directed to the single end of raising and feeding livestock. From the sale of their animals they expected to acquire the wherewithal to pay for imported goods. The first of these "banished men" took with them five kinds of beasts: swine, goats, neat cattle, sheep, and horses, which represented a heavy investment. In this respect they enjoyed a considerable advantage over the first colonists of Plymouth and the Bay. Subsequent purchases of stock in the first year or so demanded an

16. There is no record of small barns of the colony. *Winthrop Papers*, IV, 489; *Portsmouth Recs.*, 51; *The Journal of George Fox*, ed. John L. Nickalls (Cambridge, England, 1952), 622, 624; Stevens, Transcripts, II, no. 153.

17. See, in particular, Robert Trow-Smith, *A History of British Live-Stock Husbandry to 1700* (London, 1957), 84.

appreciable investment of capital, but chance—either good fortune or divine assistance—brought a sudden and precipitate drop in cattle prices after 1640 and, along with it, a cessation of imports of woolen cloth and other manufactured articles, all of which proved providential for the experiment at Rhode Island.[18]

The new plantations lived up to the expectations of the migrants. Hogs were valuable transition beasts; they could run at large in the woods and forage for themselves; so, too, could dry neat cattle survive in a country where the snows never drifted too deep. During ordinary winters even horses could subsist in the woodlands, and in very cold weather, both they and milch cows might be sheltered in the great barns. The moderate climate of the islands, in other words, combined with the security from predatory attacks to provide the region with every condition needed for successful commercial husbandry.

So easy was it to raise swine that the porker took up little space in local records. Hogs were the most numerous beasts in early Providence; both Roger Williams and John Winthrop turned their herds of swine loose to run at large on Prudence and Patience islands. In May 1639 Governor Winthrop and Richard Parke of Boston let out Prudence to John Throgmorton for three years at £40 a year and gave him £40 to stock the island with pigs. At the expiration of his lease he agreed to repay them with £40 worth of hogs. Every small farmer on Rhode Island kept some pigs, and in 1669 the inhabitants of Portsmouth, upon learning that King Philip of Mount Hope had carried several swine over to Hog Island to run at large, thereby "intrudeing on the Rights of the Towne," warned the sachem to remove all of his pigs and other cattle at once or they would proceed "to defend their Legall Rights." This insistence upon abstract rights must have puzzled as well as

18. As we read Governor Winthrop's lament of December 1640 about the economic plight at the Bay, we tend to wonder how Puritan casuists would have explained away God's manifold blessings upon the Island of Error. *Winthrop's Journal*, II, 19.

An English Barnyard, 1675

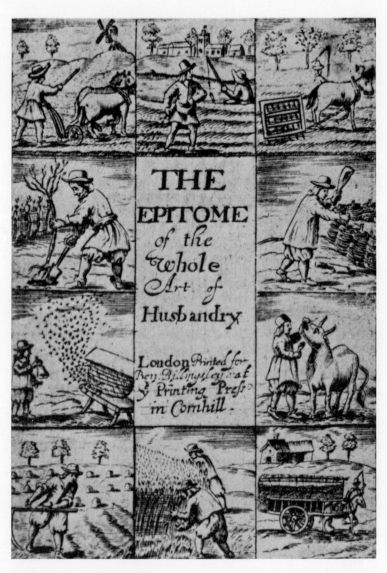

THE
EPITOME
of the
Whole
Art of
Husbandry

London Printed for
Ben: Billingsley at
ye Printing Press
in Cornhill.

Husbandmen at Work, 1685

A Rhode Island Stone-Ender, 1687

The Silver Fleece of Newport

angered the Wampanoag and added one more to his long list of grievances against the English.[19]

Hogs were seldom if ever penned, and only in special instances were they fed corn for fattening. They increased with marvelous rapidity, however, and from the first the butchers of Newport and other towns always had enough to provide hundreds of barrels of merchantable pork for Boston, Manhattan, the Chesapeake and Albemarle regions, and the West Indies. In like fashion, Rhode Island salt pork fed many a ship's crew and the fishermen off Cape Sable and Newfoundland. Pork became a staple officially after 1670 when it was accepted for both local and colony taxes at $2\frac{1}{4}d$. to $3d$. a pound; in this year at Newport "well packed pork" sold for £3 10s. a barrel. If you have any fat hogs, John Hull instructed Thomas Terry at Pettaquamscutt on October 27, 1672, slay them and salt them down, "heades and all, only cuting of[f] the feet and snoughts" and pack them for shipping. And about this time too, Benedict Arnold, Sr., charged his daughter Penelope Goulding at Taunton to have her husband bring down to Newport a barrel of salt pork, which should not be sold under £4, "for it is very thick Even as Bacon." Arnold planned to ship the pork to Barbados in the "Slope" of Providence Williams.[20]

During the first years in Rhode Island, farmers kept goats for their milk; also, a few women made goat's-milk cheese. In sending ten ewe sheep to John Winthrop, Jr., in 1649, William Almy of Portsmouth agreed to accept payment either in silver or in wether

19. *Note-Book Kept by Thomas Lechford, Esq. . . . , Archaeologia Americana*, VII (Cambridge, 1885), 68–69; *Portsmouth Recs.*, III, 148; Austin, *Genealogical Dictionary*, 23.

20. Robert Westcott deeded land and a house in the Narragansett Country in 1670 to Thomas Ward of Newport and also agreed to pay the debt of £15 to Ward "in good merchantable porke" at £3 10s. a barrel or else the deed would be voided. R.I. Land Evidences, I, 593; *Portsmouth Recs.*, 209; *R.I. Col. Recs.*, I, 359; II, 78; III, 273; John Hull, Letter Book, 1670–1685 (MS, typed copy in American Antiquarian Society, Worcester), 69; RIHS, MSS, I, Aug. 19, 1673.

goats that "will passe with the merchant[s] as silver, for I . . . am bound to pay them silver." But though goats foraged well for themselves and, like swine, made useful transition stock, the Rhode Islanders apparently decided that they had small value as an item for export, and we hear very little more of them after 1650 or, in fact, anywhere else in New England. The profits lay in cattle, sheep, and horses.[21]

NEAT cattle, as the colonists called bovines to distinguish them from other cattle (sheep, horses, swine, goats), were scarce and costly at Providence during the first years. In February 1640, before the fall in prices, even Roger Williams gratefully accepted one of the cows donated by Edward Freeman of London for the poorer colonists in return for half of the calves. The firstcomers on Aquidneck, whose chief object in going to the island was to raise livestock, brought neat cattle with them by water from Massachusetts Bay in 1638. Within two years, cattle had increased to a point that it was thought necessary at Portsmouth to create a Heraldry of the Meadows by registering the earmarks of all cattle in an official town book. By 1649 at least, cattle from Rhode Island were being shipped to Boston and Barbados. Such a stride in the raising of sizable herds had been made possible not merely by the investment of considerable sums of money by a few rich gentlemen, as Dr. Robert Child pointed out, but because these men proved to be resourceful managers of their estates.[22]

As fast as land was cleared and sowed with English grass seed, more cattle were put out to graze. Brenton, Coddington, Brinley, and others of the gentry, finding that their beef cattle were increasing at a rapid rate, divided the herds and put half of each herd

21. *Winthrop Papers*, V, 337, 344.

22. On meadow heraldry, see the earmarks shown for the cattle of Richard Bulger, John Tripp, Sr., and John Shearman in *Portsmouth Recs.*, 262, 273, 283; *Winthrop Papers*, IV, 202; *Aspinwall Recs.*, 220; R.I. Land Evidences, I, 34.

on the islands to live in the open. Dr. John Alcock and a group of Roxbury men, possibly because they observed the success achieved by the men of Aquidneck in raising cattle on their island, bought Block Island in 1661 and built a barque to transport cattle there from Braintree. Doubtless they hoped to compete in the selling of cattle to the Roxbury butchers. When Block Island became the town of New Shoreham in 1672, it was an active center for the raising of both cattle and sheep. Although Portsmouth and Newport maintained town herds for the small farmers, in other New England communities most of the cattle were pastured on the common lands. Because the cattle multiplied so fast, the General Assembly, in 1663, passed an act directing every town to build a public pound for strays under a penalty of £10 for failure to do so.[23]

The expanding Narragansett cow country underwent a major setback during King Philip's War (1675–76). From Pawtuxet the Indians drove away fifty head of William Carpenter's cattle in January 1676, and another half-hundred of "Cowkind" from the farm of William Harris's son Toleration, besides burning fifty

---

23. For readers of an urban age, it may be in order to explain the terminology used to describe the age and sex of neat cattle:

    1. The *male* is first a *bull-calf*.

    2. If it is left intact, it becomes a *bull*.

    3. If it is castrated, it becomes a *steer*, and

    4. In about two or three years grows into an *ox*.

Male bovines are assumed to fatten more readily if they are emasculated; bulls intended for working oxen are castrated, like geldings, to make them quieter and more tractable under the yoke.

    5. The *female* is first a *cow calf*.

    6. A *heifer* is a young female without a calf.

    7. The *female* which has calved is a *cow*.

    8. A *yearling* is a cow in its second year.

Encyclopaedia Britannica, 14th ed., V, 46, s.v. "Cattle-breeding." Lechford, *Note-Book*, 330–33; Samuel Livermore, *History of Block Island* [1877] (reprinted and enhanced, n.p., 1961), 16; *R.I. Col. Recs.*, I, 466, 525; *Acts and Laws of his Majesty's Colony of Rhode Island and Providence Plantations* (Newport, 1745), 13.

loads of his hay. The destruction of nearly every group of farm buildings between Providence and Point Judith, at Seekonk and Rehoboth, the driving off of all four-footed beasts, the burning of hay, and the pilfering of corn brought agricultural activity to a near standstill. As early as April 14, 1675, Increase Mather noted down that "Cattle die at Rhode Island for want of food," and within a few weeks there was another entry to the effect that many animals were starving on Long Island. Other communities, which had hitherto bought additional hay and corn on the mainland, also felt these depredations acutely. But for the relative security of the islands, the grazing industry would have been destroyed.[24]

Like most rural communities in a postwar period, the Colony of Rhode Island and Providence Plantations made a remarkable recovery after 1676. Within two years sufficient quantities of merchantable salt beef had become available to warrant accepting it for taxes at the rate of 12s. a hundred pounds, and Portsmouth rated cattle above a year old at 40s. a head in 1680. On the Narragansett shore, Kingston had been established as a self-governing town in 1674, and three years later, close upon the end of the Indian troubles, five thousand acres of land were laid out in hundred-acre tracts in the newly created town of East Greenwich, where plans had been made for stock farms by men who were moving over from Portsmouth and Newport. The arresting fact is that the first "Narragansett Planters" came from the island of Aquidneck.[25]

In the beginning the cattle brought to the Narragansett region came from Massachusetts Bay and were, in origin, of several breeds; but nearly all of them were of English stock. Under careful management on large estates, a native strain tended to emerge, because breeding could be controlled better there than it could be with the town herds that ranged on the common lands of the agrarian villages of other New England colonies. According to Adriaen

24. *RIHS Colls.*, X, 162n.; Increase Mather, *Diary* . . . , ed. Samuel A. Green (Cambridge, 1900), 42.
25. *Portsmouth Recs.*, 209; *R.I. Col. Recs.*, I, 525, 588, 599; III, 22.

van der Donck in 1656, not a few of the cattle in New Netherland had been "purchased from the English in New-England. These cattle thrive as well as the Holland cattle, and do not require much care and provender; and, as in England, this breed will do well unsheltered whole winters." They do not grow as large as the Dutch stock, he continues, but are "much cheaper" and "fat and tallow well."[26]

The very few facts that have survived do not satisfy one's curiosity about the cattle of Rhode Island, but of the prime importance of cattle to the New England economy there can be no doubt. First of all, the farmers kept a few milch cows to supply their own households with some milk to drink and more to churn for salted butter or to make into cheese. Others kept larger herds and set aside dairy rooms in their houses or erected separate outbuildings for their dairies. Tradition has it that Joan, wife of the trader Richard Smith, brought the recipe for making cheese with her from Thornbury in Gloucestershire about 1650; but cheese making was widely practiced in the days before refrigeration or where there were no springhouses in which to keep milk cool and sweet for a time. The first Rhode Islanders knew the lore of making cheese from either goat's or cow's milk when they arrived from Boston in the thirties. The inventory of Joseph Wayte of Portsmouth, who was drowned August 25, 1665, only amounted to £89 15s. 10d., which included one hundred pounds of cheese at 4d. a pound, totaling £1 13s. 4d., and ten pounds of butter listed at 5s.[27]

The bulk of the milk went into butter, however, because it was a profitable staple and could be marketed either in New England

26. Adriaen van der Donck, "Description of New Netherland," in New-York Historical Society, *Collections*, 2d ser., I, 165; Ralph A. Brown, *Historical Geography of the United States* (New York, 1948), 29–30; Percy W. Bidwell and John I. Falconer, *History of Agriculture in the Northern United States, 1620–1860* (Washington, 1925), 18–25.

27. Daniel B. Updike, *Richard Smith* ... (Boston, 1937), 22, 32; *Winthrop Papers*, V, 235; *Portsmouth Recs.*, 402.

or the West Indies. Butter shipped to the colonies from Ireland or England had to be salted, to preserve it from becoming rancid, and well packed in firkins for transport; the colonists followed the same practice with their market butter. Thus the English of the New World grew accustomed to the taste of the salted variety and have preferred it ever since to the sweet butter of Britain and Continental Europe. In 1678 "butter in the firkin" at 5*d*. a pound became acceptable for tax payments, a fact that emphasizes once more the quick recovery of the dairies after King Philip's War; and at the close of the period, Rhode Island dairy farmers made comfortable livings merely from selling firkins of butter to ship's captains and merchants.[28]

Throughout the entire colonial period, New Englanders preferred oxen to horses for draft animals, and there was no question of the superiority of these lumbering beasts for plowing or hauling or dragging on rough ground. At Newport in the 1640's, a careful distinction was made between the "cow common" and a tract of land "Comonly call'd the oxe pasture." The Providence Town Meeting agreed in 1661 that "For the Summer time upon occasion of peoples working their cattle," it would be permissible to bait them upon "the Neck." Not a few of the cattle driven overland or shipped to Boston were oxen intended for use as draft beasts on farms.[29]

In all probability the bovine population of the colony, certainly after 1660, consisted predominantly of beef cattle. From 1645 or 1650, beef, salted and fresh, became a leading item in the diet of the ordinary Rhode Islander. New Englanders of all classes regular-

28. Will of John Greene of Warwick, in *New England Historical and Genealogical Register*, V, 248–49; *R.I. Col. Recs.*, III, 22, 273; "Travel Diary of Dr. Benjamin Bullivant" [1697], in *New-York Historical Society Quarterly*, XL, 58.

29. Four oxen made "a team and two a yoke." *Providence Recs.*, III, 15, 62–63; R.I. Land Evidences, I, 34, 71.

ly ate quantities of roast beef for seventy years or more before
Richard Leveridge sang about the mythical widespread consumption of "The Roast Beef of Old England."[30]

Besides meat aplenty, the colonists obtained valuable by-products
from every part of a beef. The hides were dried, then tanned or
oiled; the result was a leather that went into shoes, clothing, gloves,
saddles, harnesses, buckets and small containers, bags and pouches,
trunks, parchment, many things for shipboard, and other goods
today not associated with leather, such as door hinges. The hard
animal fat was sold to tallow boilers who melted it from the
membranes, clarified it, and used the end product for making
candles and soap, for dressing leather, or smearing on boat and
ship bottoms to protect them against the worm. The manufacture
of cattle horns into plates, combs, and the like, almost unknown
today, was then widespread. From his own cattle and from others
raised on Rhode Island, in the Narragansett Country, and in Plymouth Colony, both at Taunton and eastward in the area around
Sandwich, as well as from the butchers of Roxbury, Charlestown,
Dedham, and Boston, John Hull acquired quantities of horns.
These Robert Cooke of Boston and other horn breakers split and
pressed into plates or fashioned into combs. During 1675 Hull
shipped four hogsheads of "pressed Hornes" and numerous barrels
of "Horne-plates" to his correspondents at London, where they
were in great demand. Returns came in nails of various sizes, much
needed for rebuilding New England after the Indian War and the
two great fires in the mart town of Boston. Here was a by-product
of the livestock industry that became a valuable staple.[31]

30. For the scarcity of meat in the average Englishman's diet before 1690,
see Carl Bridenbaugh, *Vexed and Troubled Englishmen, 1590–1640* (New
York and Oxford, 1968), 94–95.

31. In England the leather trade was said to be second only to that in
woolen cloth; in New England it must have been rivaled only by the
traffic in lumber. John Hull told his London agent that Boston horn sold

In addition to being mintmaster, treasurer of Massachusetts Bay, and a merchant, John Hull of Boston was a very active stockman, and the activities reflected from his Letter Book reveal many interesting aspects of the trade. Through his involvement with other "Boston Purchasers" and several land speculators from Rhode Island in the notorious Pettaquamscutt Purchase of 1658, he began to raise livestock on his new grazing lands. Thomas Terry became Hull's tenant-manager, and on September 4, 1672, Hull directed him to send to Boston "no Cattle but for such as are fit for sale to the bucher." The next month he wrote that had he known that Terry would be at Taunton, he would have journeyed there to speak with him about the goods and cattle Hull had given his tenant the previous year: "Yor actiones are so strangely slow and uncouth that I am sometimes Ready to doubt whether your Intentions bee right honest, as I have been willing alwayes to thinke of you." Terry ought not to have sent any cattle from Newport to Pettaquamscutt to spend the winter, and never before May. John Williams had reported to Boston, Hull said, that "you are willing to kill up the fatt Cattle of the Iland [Aquidneck], but you had no salt." The merchant shipped twelve barrels of salt to Terry by way of Providence and instructed him to kill as many fat beeves as it would preserve. All of them were to be cut into "Mess Peices" (for use on shipboard), that is, "three pound or foure at most and equally as may be." All must be good merchantable beef, Hull insisted, and Terry is not to keep out any of the best pieces, and he is not to pack any heads or "Shank bones." The barrels must be salted and filled and all the hides should be folded "smooth and handsome" and sent along with the barreled beef. Hull also directed Terry to melt the tallow into great casks, being careful not to heat it too

---

well in France. Charles Wilson, *England's Apprenticeship, 1603–1763* (London, 1965), 26; Hull, Letter Book, 42, 273, 339; *Records and Files of the Quarterly Courts of Essex County, Massachusetts*, ed. George F. Dow (Salem, 1919), VII, 259–61.

hot, so that it would be "very white." Should the supply of salt run short, he was to sell off the "unkilled remainder."[32]

Another one of John Hull's tenant-managers was William Heffernan, who turned out to be even worse than Thomas Terry. In a letter of November 8, 1672, the Bostonian marveled that Heffernan, who owed him so much, had failed to write and report to his landlord what "fall Cattle" he had at Point Judith ready for market. The complaint still held two years later when Hull demanded to know how many fattened beeves were ready, and again in 1677 when he learned that Heffernan was "so shameless" that he had offered to sell some of Hull's horses secretly. Threatening to have Heffernan arrested as a felon, the mintmaster was about ready to give up his Narragansett enterprises.[33]

The ability of swine, neat cattle, and even horses to shift for themselves in open meadows or the grovelike woodlands enabled them to survive, breed, and fatten on the islands from the very first years of settlement. But sheep need men and a supporting technology. Although their wool was a prime necessity for clothing for the colonists, sheep could not, at first, be raised in great numbers. Sheep nibble the grass so close that other four-footed animals cannot get sufficient forage if put in the same pastures. Consequently big flocks could not be raised until additional acreage was cleared or meadows drained that could be sowed with English grass seed; and this took time. The long-hidden fact that sheep raising succeeded so well in a few years is not, however, attributable entirely to the introduction of English grass. Initiative and resourcefulness

32. On John Hull, see Samuel E. Morison, *Builders of the Bay Colony* (Boston, 1930), 135–82; Hull, Letter Book, 68–69.

33. Cattle had been kept on Point Judith Neck since before 1663 when twenty-two proprietors agreed to hold it in common "for ther Drye-[beef] Cattle" by fencing it off; and in later years, Hull's son-in-law Samuel Sewall proposed the same idea for segregating horses. *The Records of the Proprietors of the Narragansett otherwise called The Fones Records* (Providence, 1894), 23–24; Hull, Letter Book, 78, 213–14, 337–38.

on the part of the planters, plus climatic conditions, contributed immeasurably.[34]

The men of Massachusetts who settled Aquidneck in 1638 brought a few sheep with them, but it was not until 1642 on Coddington's 340-acre farm, which he had leased to Jeremy Gould, that sheep raising was initiated on a large scale. Four years later, in December 1646, Dr. Robert Child estimated that there were nearly a thousand sheep on the island. This letter that William Coddington wrote on April 20, 1647, to John Winthrop, Jr., who was starting a plantation on Fishers Island, provides a rare insight into the transactions that enabled Rhode Islanders to supply ewes and rams not merely to the adjacent parts of the little colony but to Long Island and Connecticut:

"Sir, I received yours of the 17 of the present, to which I answer I intend to sell tenn ewes, most of them are as we calle them quine [queen] ewes, bringes two at a tyme, and few of them ould. Two ewes here in exchange ordenariely is given for a Cowe, and the trewth is one ewe is as much profitt to me as a Cowe. Nowe Sir my price to yow is, and under which I will not sell them, for I cann have more for them, 20 *li* in silver, English monys I desire, paid in the [Massachusetts] Baye the 20 or the 21 of June next, for then I have accation to make use of it [on a voyage to England], and then I shall within a weeke or tenn dayes after the recaite deliver tenn to mr. Smyth of newhaven (or whome yow appoynte)

34. The nomenclature of sheep (ovines):

    1. The *male* is a *ram* or *tupp*.

    2. A *wether* is a gelded male.

    3. A *ewe* is a *female* sheep after being shorn twice.

    4. A *lamb* is a young sheep, from birth until a year old.

    5. A *yearling* is a sheep in its *second year*, or its fleece.

    6. *Shearlings* are sheep of either sex shorn once or twice.

Peter J. Bowden, *The Wool Trade in Tudor and Stuart England* (London, 1962), 218; *Oxford English Dictionary*, under the terms mentioned above; *Encyclopaedia Britannica*, 11th ed., XXIV, 817–21, s.v. "Sheep."

who is to bringe me two Cottsewell [Cotswold] rambes and is to
have black ewes for them (in lifetenant Gardner['s] shalupe) if
yow take order with him accordingly, who is about that tyme to
be heare . . . in hope to procuer some sheepe for new haven. Now
Sir my desire is in the first place to pleasuer yow and because I would
not be disappoynted to answer my accations in the Baye, I desire
your speedie answer with in 14 dayes or three weekes, the sooner
the better, for I dennye secounke [Seekonk] men till I heare from
yow and alsoe New Haven and others. Ther will be no sheepe let
of[f] the Island, and those that are let are to the fowerths, for
they do ordaneriely duble in a yeare, and more for the Lambes have
Lambes when they are a yeare ould, for here is noe woolves of the
Island. . . ."[35]

Whether the ten ewes that Coddington shipped to the younger
Winthrop on October 14, 1648, were those mentioned in the
preceding letter or an additional ten is not clear. Of the latter, he
advised: "I have accordeing to your desire sent yow but tenn ewes.
They are all I doe assuer yow of the best English breed. (See
plate 4.) I could have sent yow Longe leged and biger sheepe but
these are better breed. I have sent yow five blacke and five whit. . . .
They are all but sherlings, that is one yeare ould at last lambeing,
and nowe yeening of two, which is knowne by their teeth, none
of them haveinge above two brod teeth. I have sent yow a rambe
Lambe which is of my English breed lickewise, both by the ewe
and rambe. I know the Iland nor the Cuntrie could not have
furnished yow with such a parsell of sheepe, out of my hand. . . .
If yow desire to have more whit sheepe than blacke, then rambe
your ewes with whit rambs, if more blacke, then yow may save a
black rambe out of your breed of black ewes, but by all meanes

35. For the often surprisingly different English conditions governing sheep,
see Bowden, *The Wool Trade*, chap. I: "Sheep Farming and Wool Pro-
duction." R.I. Land Evidences, I, 6g; Child to Hartlib, in *CSM Pubs.*,
XXXVIII, 51; *Winthrop Papers*, V, 149–50 (slightly edited for clarity).

put not to your rambes till the latter end of the next mounth November. . . . Richard Rayment detaynes 10*s*. 6*d*. of myne in his hand for woole you had of him."[36]

Sheep breeding and raising soon flourished in many areas of southern New England and Long Island. Coddington's letters show clearly that men in Seekonk and New Haven were in the business. A comment of John Higginson of Guilford in the New Haven Colony in 1654 is added proof that these outsiders were getting their animals from the island planters, "there being many thousands in Rhode Island, and from thence every plantation in these parts begin to get into stock more or less." One instance of the capacity of the tiny colony to supply her neighbors was a contract of 1658 by which Thomas Brookes engaged to deliver at Portsmouth before October 29 to Thomas Hawkins of Boston, butcher, "the full and just number of Fowerteene good and sownd Ewe shepe, none of them to be under the age of two yeares nor to Exceed the age of fower yeares." For prompt compliance, Brookes agreed to pledge thirty acres of land at Portsmouth, known as "the Surkitt."[37]

Although John Sanford of Newport, who died in 1653, left an estate that included many sheep, it was not until after 1660 that the marked expansion in raising sheep occurred that continued apace until the outbreak of hostilities with the Indians in 1675. After surveying the region in 1664, the Royal Commissioners notified Secretary Arlington that 'Nanhygansett Bay is the largest and safest Port in New England, nearest the Sea, and fittest for

36. In July 1648, Coddington sold John Winthrop, Jr., twenty sheep for £40, to be paid to him in England. Stephen Goodyear of New Haven inquired of Winthrop in January, 1650/1, how many sheep John Throgmorton had put on Fishers Island to graze, "and how they stand and what Encrease there is of them." The next month Goodyear reported that he had heard that the forty-five sheep on the island were John Winthrop's. *Winthrop Papers*, V, 235, 262, 269–70; VI (galleys, 25–27, in MHS).

37. Connecticut Historical Society, *Collections*, III, 319; *Portsmouth Recs.*, 352–53; RIHS, MSS, I, 35.

Trade" and added that "the best English Grass and most Sheep are in this Province, the ground being very fruitful, ewes bring ordinarily two lambs a year." Francis Brinley maintained a large flock on Conanicut, where he had acquired land in 1657. Block Island had been purchased by Roxbury projectors, and stockmen had gone there with cattle and sheep. There again the sheep multiplied prodigiously, and in 1680 the town meeting of New Shoreham ordered all sheep earmarked and registered in a second book of meadow heraldry.[38]

The expansion of the grazing of livestock from Rhode Island into eastern Long Island occurred very early. In 1648 East Hampton already possessed a great many sheep, and because they cropped the grass so close that other animals could not be put out in the same pastures, the flocks were moved out to Montauk Point. In 1678 East Hampton had fifty sheep owners with flocks numbering from 45 to 50; the total for the community was 919. A little more than ten years later, the town had 1,500 sheep in addition to its rams, and it paid a shepherd 5d. a head to watch the "General sheep flocks." Southold, by contrast, had only 90 sheep in 1680, but four years later John Budd alone owned 158.[39]

38. The lambing rate in England today varies between 1.0 and 2.0 lambs per ewe a year. "In Tudor and Stuart England lambing rates sometimes fell to 0.3, and though in good flocks they occasionally reached 0.95—as at Spindlestone in 1676—an average of 1.0 was (with the possible exception of Dorset and Wiltshire ewes) rarely, if ever achieved." Thus it appears that the Rhode Island rate was more than double that of *contemporary*, and about the same as the best *twentieth-century*, conditions in England. Bowden, *The Wool Trade*, 21–22. *New England Historical and Genealogical Register*, CIV, 304; Egerton MSS (British Museum), 2395, fols. 430b–431; Austin, *Genealogical Dictionary*, 256; *Calendar of State Papers, Colonial: America and West Indies, 1661–1668,* pp. 25, 243; R.I. Land Evidences, I, 633; Livermore, *History of Block Island*, 179–80.

39. The cost of grazing sheep on the islands was much less than on the mainland because shepherds were seldom if ever used. In contrast, Samuel Wilson reported in 1682 of the settlement on the Ashley River in Carolina:

The Rhode Islanders' success in raising sheep encouraged outsiders to invest in flocks to be pastured in their neighbors' meadows. Two Connecticut Valley men, David Wilton of Windsor and John Pynchon of Springfield, were boarding a parcel of sheep on Rhode Island "with Mr. Vaughan" in 1656. And from the Bay Town, three Hutchinsons—Samuel, Eliakim, and Elisha—all kept large flocks on Aquidneck, which their Sanford relatives looked after. Samuel's stock was pastured on the land of his nephew Samuel Sanford; in 1666 the flock contained twenty old ewes (five of them dry), two yearling wethers, one lame ram, and one lame wether. One of the Hutchinsons, probably Elisha, also kept a flock of sheep at Narragansett in that same year. Eliakim had his farm at Portsmouth where, in 1669, his tenant could dispose of twenty-two wethers.[40]

It was on Aquidneck, however, that more farmers kept sheep than anywhere else; grazing flocks, large and small, dotted the island. In 1661 the town of Portsmouth agreed to take over the care of William Baker's 102 sheep at his request when he found himself incapable of it; and while Dr. John Clarke was in England procuring the colony's charter (1662–63), his brother Thomas wintered his stock of "9 score Sheep" at Newport. To ensure proper

---

"Ewes have most commonly two or three Lambs at a time: their Wool is a good Staple and they thrive very well; but require a Shepherd to drive them to Feed, and to bring them home at night to preserve them from the Wolves." Alexander S. Salley, ed., *Narratives of Early Carolina, 1654–1708*, Original Narratives of Early American History, ed. J. Franklin Jameson (New York, 1911), 172. *Records of the Town of Easthampton, Long Island* (Sag Harbor, 1887–1905), I, *passim;* II, 236, 242; Josselyn, in *MHS Colls.*, 3d ser., III, 315; *Documents relating to the Colonial History of the State of New York*, ed. Edward B. O'Callaghan (Albany, 1856–87), XIV, 736–37; New-York Historical Society, *Collections*, 1892, pp. 131, 152.

40. *Sanford Letter Book*, 9–10, 23, 31, 32, 35–37, 60; "The Diaries of John Hull," in *Archaeologia Americana* (Boston, 1857), III, 218; John Pynchon, Account Book, ca. 1651–ca. 1694 (MSS, Connecticut Valley Historical Museum, Springfield, Mass.), V, pt. I, p. 226; RIHS, MSS, I, 60, 61.

breeding, the sheepmen of Portsmouth moved in their town meeting in 1663 that "in Consideration of the greate losses Sustained by the inhabitants of this towne, by Reson of the great Negligence in many persons, for not takeinge there Sheepe Rames from the Ewes in Seasonable time," all owners were to do so from August 10 to November 10 annually, and any rams found on the common lands during this season might be lawfully killed.[41]

From the outset, the raising of large flocks of sheep for export remained in the hands of men of substance who were both stock-breeders and merchants. Governor William Brenton was undoubtedly the leading grazier of New England when he died at Taunton in 1674. To his children he bequeathed six farms in Plymouth, Massachusetts Bay (on the Merrimack), besides several Rhode Island, Conanicut, and Narragansett holdings. At Hammersmith Farm in Newport and two or three other farms all leased to tenants, there were 1,613 sheep at the time of his death. The worth of his entire estate was set at £10,768 13s. 4d. Even in Britain he would have been thought a rich man. Much closer to the average farm on Rhode Island was that of old Richard Borden of Portsmouth, who died three years before Brenton. He left to his Quaker heirs thirty ewe sheep and fifty others, as well as three cows and three pigs. But whether the flocks of Aquidneck and the other islands were great or small, one cannot question the assertion of William Harris that there were more sheep in Rhode Island than anywhere else in New England. He concluded with understandable local pride that it was "the Garden of New-England."[42]

During the years 1675–76, Indian enemies killed or drove off nearly all of the livestock of the mainland farmers. When they raided the Pawtuxet farm of William Carpenter, they took away

41. *Portsmouth Recs.*, 101, 119–20, 181; Horace E. Turner, comp., Colonial Land Evidences (Rhode Island), [MS, NHS] bk. I, 33.

42. I have used the original of William Brenton's will (Brenton-Mulford MSS, NHS), box 5; Austin gives a good summary, *Genealogical Dictionary*, 23, 254; R.I. Land Evidences, I, 431–34; *RIHS Colls.*, X, 144.

180 sheep besides his cattle and horses. Aquidneck, Conanicut, Block, and the smaller islands remained fairly safe for men and beasts, and when the war ended, their graziers were able and willing to supply breeding sheep to the farmers of their colony, Plymouth, Connecticut, and Massachusetts Bay, with the result that a vastly increased demand for sheep set in and stimulated the expansion of pastureland that had been interrupted by the hostilities.[43]

When ships stopped arriving after 1641, the shortage of clothing gave a strong impetus to the growing of flax and the raising of sheep, for the weaving of cloth for garments needed by rural New Englanders became a necessity. John Higginson, some years later, reassured the Reverend Thomas Thatcher in the Bay that "God seems to provide in a gradual way for supply in clothing by the multiplying of sheep." And two years later in 1656, Adriaen van der Donck reported that his colony did not have nearly as many sheep as did New England, "where the weaving business is driven, and where much attention is paid to sheep." An official recognition of the New Englanders' ability to take care of themselves in this matter appears in a report to the Council for Foreign Plantations about the growth of New England during the Civil Wars. Messrs. Howe and Noell stated with some alarm on April 30, 1661, that the colonists had "increased a Stock of Sheepe to the number of neere one hundred thousand Sheepe, whereby, not only this Nation and the manufacture thereof are become less necessary to them, but they are likely to be so stored with wool that the Dutch, who trade freely with them, may supply themselves from thence."[44]

Customarily historians of American agriculture celebrate the introduction of Merino sheep after 1800 to the almost total exclusion of all that had gone before. For seventeenth-century New England, the truth is that the fleeces of Rhode Island–bred "sheep's

43. *RIHS Colls.*, X, 162n.; 163.

44. Connecticut Historical Society, *Collections*, III, 319; New-York Historical Society, *Collections*, 2d ser., I, 166; Egerton MSS (British Museum), 2395, fol. 299; RIHS, MSS, I, 35, 60.

wool, well washed, good and merchantable" proved to be a more than adequate staple for the weaving both of all-wool cloth or linsey-woolsey, which was a mixture of wool and flax. Messrs. Howe and Noell had foretold in 1661 that the Hollanders might take as much of this wool as they would need "to mingle with their finer Wools, which they would draw together out of several parts of Europe." Nevertheless the fleeces produced on the good meadows of Rhode Island and Providence Plantations were superior to those clipped anywhere else in New England. Although the number seems unduly large today, it is possible that the colony did contain the two hundred thousand sheep that La Mothe Cadillac was told it had in 1692, for it would represent only the doubling of the flocks since 1661. There is no doubt whatever that the colony did have more sheep than any other English colony by a considerable margin and that they constituted a very large share of its wealth. Appropriately enough, when Arnold Collins, the silversmith, made an ivory-handled, silver "Seal of Newport Rhoad Island Councel" in 1696, the device was a sheep statant. (See plate 4.) [45]

HORSES were one more kind of beast that the stock farmers of Rhode Island bred for a profitable export. They also could be allowed to graze in open fields or meadows in spring, summer, and fall and to seek fodder in the woods where there was little underbrush in the winter, although, as John Josselyn observed, they were "very low in flesh" by spring. At first they were raised for riding or for use as pack animals on the crude paths and roads, not for

45. See, again, Bowden, *The Wool Trade*, index, s.v. "Wool." The Newport seal is in the Newport Historical Society. In 1672, when Conanicut was incorporated as Jamestown, the residents adopted for their seal a shield with a green field surmounted by a white [an ermine] sheep. Howard M. Chapin and Norman Isham, *Illustrations of the Seals, Arms, and Flags of Rhode Island* (Providence, 1930), 6, 57; *Portsmouth Recs.*, 352–54; Egerton MSS (British Museum), 2395, fol. 299; La Mothe Cadillac, in Maine Historical Society, *Collections*, VI, 288.

draft, though at Providence some persons employed them to pull two-wheeled carts or plows. Running wild for the most part, the horses bred indiscriminately and increased rapidly.[46]

Astute in sensing opportunities for trade and resourceful in implementing their ideas, William Brenton and William Coddington undertook in 1647 to breed stallions and mares with the object of selling them to the sugar planters of Barbados, some for riding, but primarily for turning the sugar mills. They disposed of a few of them to sugar planters, and they also found some purchasers in the Bay Colony. But it was not until after the English government set a duty in 1654 on all horses exported from Britain that the New Englanders had a lucrative market to exploit. In 1656 Coddington was arranging to ship sixteen horses to Barbados from Boston, and at the same time Roger Kilvert sailed up from Manhattan to buy horses at Newport or "Warrack" for breeding in New Netherland. Political difficulties notwithstanding, Thomas Minor and other men of eastern Connecticut made periodic trips to the Narragansett Country from 1662 onward to buy breeding mares and colts. In the sixties horses began to rival hogs, neat cattle, and sheep as a leading staple of Rhode Island.[47]

46. Josselyn, in *MHS Colls.*, 3d ser., III, 338; *Providence Recs.*, VI, 19, 73.

47. Concerning the Barbadian sugar mills in 1648, Sir Edmund Plowden wrote: ". . . New England sendeth Horses, and Virginia Oxen, to turn them at excessive rates." "A Description of the Province of New Albion . . ." (London, 1648), in Peter Force, ed., *Tracts and other Papers Relating Principally to . . . North America* (Washington, 1836), II, no. 7, p. 5; Carl and Roberta Bridenbaugh, *No Peace Beyond the Line: The English in the Caribbean, 1624–1690* (New York, 1972), 97; Nathaniel B. Shurtleff, ed., *Records of the Governor and Company of Massachusetts Bay in New England* (Boston, 1853), II, 190; Massachusetts Archives: Agriculture (MSS, State House, Boston), I, 12; *Aspinwall Recs.*, 32; Helen Capewell, ed., *Records of the Court of Trials of the Colony of Providence Plantations* (Providence, 1920), I, 19–20; Berthold Fernow, ed., *Records of New Amsterdam, 1655–1663* (New York, 1902), II, 79; Sidney H. Minor and G. D. Stanton, eds., *The Diary of Thomas Minor of Stonington, Connecticut, 1653–1684* (New London, 1899), 47, 49, 50, 52.

In the course of describing New England for Fleetwood Shepheard at London in 1675, William Harris said of his own colony that Rhode Island was "healthy and well replenished with people and cattle, and so many horses that men know not what to do with them." This situation was demonstrably true of Portsmouth, for at that very time the town meeting found it necessary to restrict each household to pasturing but one horse above a year old on the common lands between April 1 and October 1, and it had to be "well fettered." On Conanicut the equine population was gaining on that of sheep in 1681; but the greatest increment came in the Narragansett Country, which, in the eighteenth century, would become the leading horse raising area of all New England. John Hull, in 1677, had sought to persuade Governor Benedict Arnold and his partners in the Pettaquamscutt Purchase to fence off Point Judith Neck as a horse preserve so that "no mongrel breed" might come among them, for he wanted to develop "a very choise breed for coach-horses, some for the saddle, some for draught." He tried to convince them that in a few years they might be able to ship off "considerable numbers . . . for Barbados, Nevis," and other sugar islands. He also hoped to have a special vessel made for that service. A most unusual solution was taken by the court to relieve the new town of Rochester (Kingston), which was being disturbed by the "many wild horses of two years old or upwards." Of these, "30 or fewer" were to be taken up and sold, and the proceeds were to be used to build a prison and stocks.[48]

No person knew more about early New England than Samuel Maverick, who perceived quite clearly by 1660 that a marked transition had occurred in that region in about thirty-five years. "And for the Southern part of New-England. It is incredible what hath been done there [in Rhode Island and Connecticut and on

48. *Calendar of State Papers, Colonial, 1675–1676*, p. 213; *Portsmouth Recs.*, 189; Austin, *Genealogical Dictionary*, 39; Hull, Letter Book, 336; *R.I. Col. Recs.*, III, 202.

Long Island]. In the yeare 1626 or thereabouts there was not a Neat Beast, Horse or sheape in the Countrey and a very few Goats or hoggs, and now it is a wonder to see the great herds of Cattle belonging to every Towne. . . . The brave Flocks of Sheape. The great number of Horses besides those many sent to Barbados and other Carribe Islands, and withall to consider how many thousand Neat Beasts and Hoggs are yearly killed, and soe have been for many years past for Provision in the Countrey and sent abroad to supply Newfoundland, Barbados, Jamaica, and other places, and also to victuall in whole or in part most ships which comes there." Thirty years after this statement by Maverick, the denizens of Naboth's Meadows had doubled or trebled their numbers and had forced a notable growth of commerce and shipping in Rhode Island and Providence Plantations.[49]

49. The fishermen of Rhode Island do not appear to have engaged in commercial fishing; they did, however, supply the local market regularly. Learning from the Cape Cod and Long Island fishermen about offshore whaling, they took to it some time after 1647, and the earliest detailed account of the pursuit of a whale along the New England coast that is known is given in full in Appendix V. Maverick, in *MHS Procs.*, 2d ser., I, 247.

IV

THE QUAKER
GRANDEES OF
RHODE ISLAND

THE swift course of unanticipated events made the year 1657 even more of a turning point in the history of Rhode Island and Providence Plantations than the charter year of 1663. More than ever the economic, social, and political destiny of the little colony hinged upon the continued maintenance of liberty of conscience. Attempts by outsiders to appropriate all or part of Naboth's Meadows by stirring up factions among the settlers failed, but some of the land-hungry men achieved their goal by collaborating with several Rhode Islanders in acquiring extensive tracts of rich grazing land from the Narragansett Indians. Negotiations for the notorious Pettaquamscutt Purchase were under way in 1657. Concurrently ill-concealed commercial pressure from neighboring colonies drove merchants in the harassed community to seek out friendly traders elsewhere; their influence or case was such that on May 19 the General Assembly resolved that "the Dutch may have lawfull commerce with the English in this Collony, correspondent to the peace in beinge betweene the nations."[1]

1. The next year, on May 18, the General Assembly forbade the seizure of any Dutch ship in Narragansett waters unless "by an express and especiall commission from the state of England" or by "the law-making Assembly of this Collonie." Patently these measures were to protect the coastal trade with Manhattan that was so vital to the survival of Rhode Island. *R.I. Col. Recs.*, I, 356, 389. Besides the extensive Pettaquamscutt and Atherton (1659) land-grabs in the Narragansett Country, Boston merchants acquainted with

The ship *Woodhouse* of London, but last from New Amsterdam, landed a missionary band of the Society of Friends at Newport on August 3, 1657. In June of the previous year, the arrival of several Quakers from Barbados had set Boston in an uproar; now the Commissioners of the United Colonies of New England, meeting in the Bay Town, learned of the presence of the "apostles" at Rhode Island and thought it "meet to manifest theire minds to the Governor there" that they "thinke noe care too great to preserve us from such a pest, the contagion whereof (if received) within your Collonie were dangerous . . . to be defused to the other by means of the intercourse, especially the place of trade amongst us." This letter continued, making the "request" of the Rhode Islanders that they "remove those Quakers that have been receaved" and prohibit any others from entering in the future. They also hinted ominously that "it will bee our duty seriously to consider what further provision God may call us to make to prevent the aforesaid mischiefe." Humorlessly unaware, no doubt, of the insolence of this threat of retaliation, the commissioners arrogantly demanded a reply of concurrence by the time of the meeting of the General Court of Massachusetts on October 14. The answer of the General Assembly was signed by its clerk on October 13; that the copy of this document signed and sent by Governor Benedict Arnold to the commissioners, and not to the General Court, reached Boston the next day seems highly improbable.[2]

Governor Arnold was both polite and conciliatory in his reply and sought to allay the patent fears of men in other colonies, but

---

the favorable economic conditions were buying in cleared farms and tracts of land from 1657 to 1690 on Aquidneck, Block, and Prudence islands. See *R.I. Land Evidences*, I, *passim*.

2. Rufus Jones, *The Quakers in the American Colonies* (New York, 1966), 51, 53; *R.I. Col. Recs.*, I, 374–78. The Assembly's answer on October 13, signed by John Sanford and addressed to Governor John Endecott for the United Colonies, is in Rhode Island Colony Records, 1646–1669 (MS, R.I. Archives), 123–24.

courtesy did not obscure principle, which he elucidated with exquisite irony:

"And as concerning these quakers (so called), which are now among us, we have no law among us, whereby to punish any for only declaring by words, etc. their mindes and understandings concerning the things and ways of God, as to salvation and an eternal condition. And we, moreover, finde, that in those places where these people aforesaid, in this coloney, are most of all suffered to declare themselves freely, and are only opposed by arguments in discourse, there they least of all desire to come, and we are informed that they begin to loath this place, for that they are not opposed by the civill authority but with all patience and meeknes are suffered to say over their pretended revelations and admonitions, nor are they like or able to gain many here to their way." In closing he promised "to commend the consideration of their extravagant outgoings" to the General Assembly that would convene in March 1657/8.[3]

The "request" of the commissioners was duly reviewed by the assembly at its March meeting. Undoubtedly all the members of this body understood fully that the existence of their colony was precarious at best and that a refusal to comply with the demands of the United Colonies about Quakers would bring them little but trouble. Nevertheless the assembly, couching its reply in civil terms, stated frankly that "freedom of different consciences to be protected from Inforcements was the principle [sic] ground of our Charter" from Parliament in 1644 and that it would abide by both the spirit and the letter of that instrument.[4]

---

3. Among Boston Puritans, John Hull at least conceded the validity of Benedict Arnold's view of the Quakers: "They seem to suffer patiently, and take a kind of pleasure in it. In those parts of the country where they might with freedom converse (as in Rhode Island and Providence and Warwick), they take no pleasure to be." "The Diaries of John Hull," in *Archaeologia Americana* (Boston, 1857), III, 182. *R.I. Col. Recs.*, I, 376–78.

4. In 1658 a few Sephardic Jews, probably from Barbados, came to live in

It soon became apparent that the commissioners' threat was not an idle one, for on November 3–4 of that same year, 1658, a letter went out to Dr. John Clarke, the agent for Rhode Island in London, to inform him not only of the offensive attitude taken by these unfriendly neighbors but of actual harassment. The commissioners, it was pointed out, "seeme seacretly to threaten us, by cuttinge us off from all commerce and trade with them and thereby to disable us of any comfortable subsistence, being that the concourse of shippinge, and soe of all kinds of comodities is universally conversant amongst themselves; as also knowinge that ourselves are not in a capacity to send out shippinge of ourselves, which is in a great measure occasioned by their oppressinge of us as yourselfe well knowes; as in many other respects, soe in this for one, that wee cannot have any thinge from them for the suply of our necessities, but in efect they make the prices, both of our commodities, and their own also, because wee have not English coyne, but only that which passeth amonge these barbarians, and such comodities as are raised by the labour of our hands, as corne, catell, tobbacco, and the like, to make payment in, which they will have at their own rate, or else not deal with us. Whereby (though *they gaine extraordinarily by us*), yett for the safeguard of their own religion may seem to neglect themselves in that respect; for what will men doe for their God."[5]

The authorities at Plymouth, following the lead of their colleagues at the Bay, also applied economic pressure to their designated enemies, the Friends. James Cudworth, lately a magistrate, asserted that in December 1658, "Some of the Quakers from Road Island came to bring them goods to trade with them [at Sandwich and Cape Cod], and that for far reasonabler terms, then the professing, oppressing Merchants of the Country, but that will not be suffered, [and] that unless the Lord step in to their help and

Newport; more had arrived by 1677 when they acquired land for a burial place. Morris A. Gutstein, *The Story of the Jews of Newport* (New York, 1936), 30–31, 341–42; *R.I. Col. Recs.*, I, 378–80.

5. *R.I. Col. Recs.*, I, 396–98 (italics mine).

assistance some way beyond mans conceiving, their case is sad and to be pitied. . . ." Some months later, because Plymouth appeared too lenient in persecuting Quakers, Cudworth exclaimed: "We expect that we must do the like, we must dance after their Pipe: Now [that the] Plymouth-Saddle is upon the Bay-Horse. . . ."[6]

The authorities of the United Colonies underestimated the abilities and stamina of the inhabitants of the "Island of Error." Even Governor Arnold turned out to be mistaken about the Quakers' loathing the place; so compatible, in fact, and in many ways so alike were the religious views of the Hutchinson Antinomians and those of the followers of George Fox that the former were, as Rufus Jones once observed, already "Quakers in everything but name." And before 1665, such leading inhabitants of Aquidneck as Coddington, the Bordens, Eastons, Goulds, Coggeshalls, and Clarkes, Henry Bull, Henry Beare, the Fosters and Freeborns declared themselves "convinced Friends." After 1676, the now-familiar names of Hodgson, Colson, Thurston, Cullen, Motte, and Cornell also appear in the records of the Newport Monthly Meeting. From Boston came Edward Shippen to join the Friends in Newport as did the Wantons from Scituate, the brothers John and Thomas Rodman, physicians of Barbados, and Walter Newbury of London. Many hundreds of lesser folk—farmers, artisans, mariners, fishermen, and their families followed those whom Sir Edmund Andros dubbed "the Quaker Grandees of Rhode Island." From 1672 to 1677 the Friends controlled the government of the colony, and frequently thereafter one of their number occupied the office of governor. Close to one-half of the population of the colony in 1690 belonged to the Society of Friends.[7]

6. John Rous, *New England a Degenerate Plantation* (London, 1659), 16, 20.

7. William Harris, in a description of the New England governments for an English official, wrote in 1675: "The Governor of Rhode Island, Codington, theyr Deputy Easton, Assistants Bull, Gould, Clark, Coggeshall, Trip, Harris, Allmy, Barton, some of them called Quakers, some Called Generalles"

Thus, beginning in the year 1657, what had long been a local Antinomian problem on Aquidneck was being rapidly transformed and expanded into an intercolonial—even imperial—Quaker issue. Within four years "a very great" yearly meeting for New England assembled for four days at Newport; and, also by 1661, Quakers had set up a monthly meeting at Sandwich in Plymouth Colony, and many people of southeastern Massachusetts and Plymouth were being "convinced" by traveling Friends who rode out from the two centers at Newport and Sandwich. Edward Wharton went with some companions from Salem to the Piscataqua region in 1662, where they began to win over many former adherents of John Wheelwright and Anne Hutchinson, as well as the powerful merchant Nicholas Shapleigh (Shapley) of Kittery.[8]

One of the first to be convinced in the Old Colony was Nicholas Davis; and he was expelled from Boston when he went there to trade in 1659. Even before the arrival of George Fox, this merchant of Hyannis on the south shore of Cape Cod had been striving with marked success to link the new communities of Friends in Plymouth, Rhode Island, and New York with the New World Quaker base at Barbados by means of commerce and shipping. He trafficked with the Dutch from his warehouse on his large farm at Hyannis, and in 1662–63 he was shipping horses from Newport to Barbados in the ketch *Tryall* owned by its Quaker master, Thomas Richardson. When the English conquered New Netherland, Davis kept one or more vessels of his own sailing from Hyannis and Rhode Island to New York. He moved to Newport in 1669 and extended his ventures to Virginia and, it was said, to Holland; he was,

---

[and none either Anglican or Congregationalist]. Roger Williams called Harris "a doleful Generalist" before he became a Quaker. Gay Collection of Transcripts relating to the History of New England, 1630–1776 (MHS), V, 40–41; Society of Friends [Newport] Monthly Meeting Minutes, 1676–1707 (MS, RIHS), *passim;* Jones, *Quakers,* xv, 24–25.

8. Jones, *Quakers,* 54, 57*n.*, 58, 62, 103–5; *MHS Colls.,* 4th ser., IX, 155–56; Frederick B. Tolles, *Quakers and the Atlantic Culture* (New York, 1960).

incidentally, the master of the sloop that carried George Fox from Oyster Bay to Newport in May 1672. Davis was drowned in Newport Harbor late in July 1672, and, since he had left no will, his landed estate at Whitestone, Long Island, and house in Smith's Fly in New York had to be disposed of by the Executive Council in New York sitting as a court. On this occasion, Governor Francis Lovelace referred to Nicholas Davis as one "Whose active Spirit for the promotion of a public Interest will now appear a great Loss." Such praise for a Quaker from a member of the established faith of England was indeed praise from Sir Hubert.[9]

The greatest expansion of Quakerism in New England followed close upon the visit of George Fox and his labors in the Rhode Island colony from late May to July 1672. In June, a memorable yearly meeting, attended by Fox and several eminent English Friends, William Coddington, Governor Nicholas Easton, and other public officials, attracted a concourse of Quakers from all over New England—Massachusetts Bay, New Hampshire, the province of Maine, Plymouth, and Long Island, besides Rhode Island and Providence Plantations. Steady habits must have kept the Connecticut people away. When the sessions ended it was thought that those persons attending needed two days to settle affairs of business and take leave of each other; "And yet by the continued coming in of people in sloops from divers other colonies and jurisdictions it continued longer, and for several days we had large meetings."[10]

George Fox worked diligently and effectively in setting up monthly meetings at Providence and Narragansett and on Shelter

9. Jones, *Quakers*, 79; William and Thomas Richardson, Account Book, 1662–1702 (MS, NHS), s.v. 1663–1664; Victor H. Paltsits, ed., *Minutes of the Executive Council of the Province of New York* (Albany, 1910), I, 165*n*.; II, 773–89.

10. *The Journal of George Fox*, ed. John L. Nickalls (Cambridge, England, 1952), 620–21; *MHS Procs.*, 2d ser., III, 258; Henry J. Cadbury, "Intercolonial Solidarity of American Quakerism," in *Pennsylvania Magazine of History and Biography*, LX, 363–69.

Island, where he discovered "a great desire there is among the people." He arranged further for regular men's and women's meetings "in all of the colonies." On July 25, 1672, this leader boldly urged the public officials of Rhode Island to adopt practicable proposals at once for the common weal. Ardently he called for passage of a law against drunkenness, of a second against fighting and swearing, and a third to set up a weekly market and provide for the erection of a market house. He advised also the careful recording in a book in every town of all births, marriages, and deaths, as he had insisted upon in all other Quaker communities. With true wisdom, George Fox urged that "all your ancient Liberties [be] looked into and Priviledges and agreements concerning your Divine Liberty and Nationall Liberty, and *all your outward liberties and priviledges of your Comons that belong to your Towne, Island, and Colony . . . be looked into.*"[11]

In addition to organizing and charging all New England Friends to work in unity for political, social, and economic betterment, Fox saw to it that several meetings of the region and the central Yearly Meeting at London were kept regularly in touch by means of epistles exchanged annually or oftener. And while he was a guest in the house of William Coddington at Newport, he told of Samuel Winthrop's activities in Barbados and Antigua, as well as those of Lewis Morris and other insular Friends. At his departure in August 1672, this dynamic leader left the Quakers of New England not just a tightly knit organization for divine worship and charitable enterprise but one in close communication with the Friends of Barbados, Ireland, and England.[12]

11. Thomas Olney, Jr., of Providence and others resented the didacticism of Fox and, on June 5, 1673, circulated a scornful critique: Ambition Anatomized, Or, Considerations upon some Instructions Given forth by G. ff in a paper bearing the Date of the 25th of the 5th Mo: 1672, in Rhode Island. Fox's letter and this reply are in RIHS, MSS, I, no. 26 (italics mine); Fox, *Journal*, 623–26.

12. For the activities of Samuel Winthrop and Lewis Morris in Barbados

The genius George Fox displayed in organizing the Society of Friends for religious action, which ensured their solidarity in the face of all detractors, has often been commented upon; but the possibilities of using yearly, quarterly, monthly, weekly, and special meetings to foster trade and other aspects of the material welfare of widely scattered Friends, particularly in New England, have been overlooked. One can scarcely overemphasize the effectiveness of Fox's Quaker network for purposes of trade and commerce. Through the meetings of Friends, the grandees of Rhode Island succeeded in marketing their agricultural surpluses profitably to other Friends located along the Atlantic Coast, in the West Indies, and in the British Isles, thereby rescuing the farmers and graziers of the Narragansett region from absolute dependence upon the Puritan caprices of Boston traders.

GRAZING and the culture of Indian corn were flourishing in Rhode Island and Providence Plantations when the Quakers arrived in 1657, and a small, though steadily mounting, surplus of hogs, cattle, sheep, and maize was being shipped out for sale at Boston and New Amsterdam. This traffic had been managed by fewer than a dozen men of substance, who combined their agricultural with mercantile and maritime pursuits. In the fifties the band of Antinomian founders had been augmented by the Anglican Francis Brinley from Barbados, Dutch Laed Strengs "free Merchant" of Manhattan, and Richard Smith, the Puritan from Cocumscussoc across Narragansett Bay. For the most part, they dispatched their produce to market in Dutch or Massachusetts bottoms, using their own small craft for trading with nearby Connecticut, New Haven, Cape Cod, and eastern Long Island.[13]

---

and Antigua, see Carl and Roberta Bridenbaugh, *No Peace Beyond the Line: The English in the Caribbean, 1624–1690* (New York, 1972), 357–59, 386–93, 397–98, and index; *MHS Colls.*, 4th ser., VII, 288.

13. In their unrelenting urge to acquire land, these merchants, like those of the Bay, were acting as their class always had acted for centuries. Roger

Those who became convinced Friends were soon joined by
Quaker merchants from other parts who recognized the commer-
cial promise of Newport. The newcomers, enjoying excellent
family and denominational trading connections with distant ports,
proceeded energetically after 1660 to organize the economy of
their chosen home. Dr. John Clarke, a Baptist, procured the pre-
cious Charter of 1663 from King Charles II, who gave the little
colony an unassailable legal existence, negotiable if not fixed bound-
aries, valuable economic guarantees, and ensured religious freedom.
To the very great credit of the Society of Friends, its members
willingly associated with those other merchants who, according
to William Harris, "in all the Colonyes" of New England were
called "Common Protestants"—Baptists, Anglicans, Congregation-
alists, and Seventh-Day Baptists. Before long they had their mer-
cantile agents stationed at strategic points along the periphery of
the Atlantic basin; and, following the visit of George Fox, they
utilized with notable skill the far-flung organization of the Society
of Friends for promoting trade.[14]

The precise ways and means by which the Friends worked out
an intricate system to counter in trade, quite as much as in worship,
the long-established Yankee network is both intriguing and en-
lightening. The apostate Friend, George Keith, in 1702 listed first
among twenty-four ways by which the Friends supported their
many activities "their Established Weekly, Monthly, Quarterly,
and yearly Meetings." On such occasions they indulged in "great
hospitality to all friends, and others" who came to their public

---

Williams understood this when he wrote an often-misunderstood letter to
John Winthrop, Jr., in 1664: "I fear that the common trinity of the world
(Profit, Preferment, Pleasure) will here be the *Tria omnia*, as in all the
world beside: that Prelacy and Popery too in this wilderness predominate;
that God Land will be (as now it is) as great a God with us English as God
Gold was with the Spaniards, etc." *Narr. Club Pubs.*, VI, 319; Holland
Society of New York, *Year Book* (New York, 1900), XIII, 180.

14. *RIHS Colls.*, X, 146.

meetings, "especially their Quarterly and Yearly Meetings." They saw to it that Fox's "Orders and Canons" were "duly and orderly read in the Monthly and especially the Quarterly Men's and Women's Meetings." By these and other means, the Quakers succeeded in "keeping their Trade within themselves and maintaining a strict Correspondence and Intelligence over all parts where they are."[15]

Such procedures have been branded a Quaker innovation. But from the time of the rise of cities in the later Middle Ages, trade had been carried on for safety's sake within the groups deemed most trustworthy, family and national, by the merchants of a given town or region. Boston traders were using family connections in England and elsewhere in precisely the same way and at the same time that the Quaker merchants were going them one better by trading simultaneously within their families and within the membership of the Society by corresponding and working through their meetings. Neither the merchants among "the Saints of New England" nor those of the Friends were doing aught but employing hoary medieval methods of trade. The acerbic taunt that the Quakers have always had one foot in the meetinghouse and the other in the countinghouse historically applies equally to Roman Catholics, Jews, and Puritans.[16]

As a group the merchants, headed by Quakers, recognized and understood the agricultural-commercial-maritime nature of their economy and went about organizing and managing life and labor in the colony in keeping with it. By 1690 they had come quietly to control not alone all agrarian pursuits but, in like manner, the arts and crafts, the lumbering industry, shipbuilding, overland transport, and water-borne trade, whether local, coastal, or "foreign." As they accumulated more wealth than they could or wished to risk

15. Keith, in Protestant Episcopal Historical Society, *Collections*, I, xix–xx.
16. Frederick B. Tolles, *Meeting House and Counting House: The Quaker Merchants of Colonial Philadelphia* (Chapel Hill, 1948), viii.

in cargoes and ships, they adopted the age-old course of investing it in additional acres. Like the "Saints" and other "Common Protestants," these merchants had one foot in the Middle Ages and the other in the seventeenth century—in modern times.[17]

By electing members of their own class as deputies and as governor between 1672 and 1676, the Friends controlled the government of the colony and were able to enact most of their ideas and proposals into law. During the perilous years 1675 and 1676, in the face of savage criticism from the commissioners of the United Colonies, they managed to remain noncombatants while still rendering timely nonmilitary aid and charitable assistance to many refugees. Small wonder, then, that no tears were shed on Rhode Island or in Providence Plantations when the Crown vacated the Massachusetts Bay Company's charter in 1684. Without incident, the Rhode Islanders quietly accepted the authority of Joseph Dudley in September 1685, and when Sir Edmund Andros united the northern colonies as the Dominion of New England in 1686, the Epistle of the Rhode Island Yearly Meeting to the London Friends of August 27 expressed the sardonic satisfaction of the Quakers all over New England that they now were on the same plane religiously with the Puritans of the defunct New England Confederation, who had treated them in such an unchristian fashion since 1656. To which they might have added that, within the Dominion of New England, they now also enjoyed unrestricted freedom of trade.[18]

17. For a partial list of men of the Narragansett region, each of whom was always referred to as a "merchant," see Appendix III.

18. As far back as February 1674/5, an unnamed Massachusetts mariner had written to Boston from Barbados that many people there who envied the prosperous state of New England were saying that "all will bee reduced under New Yorke, a thing the Quakers heere much long for. . . ." *MHS Procs.*, VII, 16; Rhode Island Yearly Meeting, Epistle, August 27, 1686, in Epistles Received (Friends Library, London), I, 21, as cited by David Lovejoy, *The Glorious Revolution in America* (New York, 1972), 193; George Keith, *A Refutation of Three Opposers of Truth* . . . (Philadelphia, 1690), 64.

IN their roles as merchants and stockmen, the grandees of Rhode Island had a large stake in attracting, encouraging, patronizing, and financing the artisans who worked at the arts and trades auxiliary to farming and shipping. They illustrated nicely George Keith's twenty-second explanation of how the Quakers supported their activities: "By the People's great liberality to all their Itinerant Preachers, and putting their Ministers generally into a way of Trade, especially Merchandizing, and putting many poor Mechanics, Servants, and Women, that have no good way of living . . . into such ways of Trade and business, whereby to live plentifully, by which means, many who had nothing are become rich." Between 1660 and 1690 at Newport, Portsmouth, and Providence, artisans and craftsmen found work in many trades, whereas in the countryside many of them combined farming with the exercise of their chosen mysteries.[19]

From the sources used for this volume, it has been possible to compile a list of more than a hundred artisans and tradesmen who worked at twenty-seven separate crafts, each of them closely related to the commercial agriculture of the colony. More than a quarter of these men engaged in work having to do with forest industries or woodworking. Trees felled in clearing the ground for planting or grazing supplied them with their raw material: heavy house or barn timbers and lighter posts and rails for fences. As Newport grew in population from three hundred in 1650 to about two thousand by 1690, axmen cut up the smaller stuff for fuel for households, whose increasing numbers presented a mounting demand. Another useful forest product was tar, which was used for caulking seams in ships and boats and for marking sheep and dressing cuts inflicted in shearing; it also found a ready sale in the Caribbean. The inhabitants of Providence rejected several schemes in 1681 to draw off tar and burn wood for charcoal because of "the Great Benefit they have had by there pitchwod for Candell

19. Keith, in Protestant Episcopal Historical Society, *Collections*, I, xx.

light"; up until 1689, when "the use of Baywax came to be publick-ly knowne" at Newport, pitchwood and tallow candles provided nearly all of the illumination.[20]

Building created an unprecedented demand for wood to be made into beams, joists, boards, clapboards, shingles, and all sorts of casks, so that in time a critical shortage developed. Logs of large diameter were sent to sawyers to be cut into boards, and even before 1650 Plymouth officials complained bitterly that woodsmen from Rhode Island went up the Taunton River to fell trees on the common lands there and conveyed them downstream to their own sawyers and mills. This poaching on their preserves encouraged the men of Taunton to build a sawmill of their own in 1659. In the ensuing years more mills were constructed. Just below Pawtucket Falls, Joseph Jenckes erected a sawmill in 1672; it was burned down during the Indian War, but he had it rebuilt and working again in 1679. John Scott of Providence and Richard Arnold of James-town built a sawmill in partnership on the Moshassuck River in 1673 to saw logs brought down that stream from the hinterland of Providence. The emergency arising after the burning of houses and farm buildings by the Indians swelled the demand, and when the old mill on Tuskatucket Brook in Warwick proved inadequate in 1676, four men established a new sawmill the next year on the Pawtuxet River. For some time before his death in 1682, John Smith managed a sawmill at Providence; and to supply Aquidneck with sawn boards by a convenient outlet down the Warren River, Timothy Brooks received permission to set up a sawmill at Swan-sea in 1681. Observable inroads were made in the woodlands and forests of the entire region in order to furnish all of the wood necessary to replace the virtually total loss of housing and furnish-

20. See Appendix IV for a list of crafts and craftsmen. Egerton MSS (British Museum), 2395, fol. 70; *Providence Recs.*, VIII, 102–4; *Magazine of New England History*, III, 203; Carl Bridenbaugh, *Cities in the Wilderness* (New York, 1955), 6.

ings on the mainland. By 1690 the colonists were having to go far afield for wide boards and sound ship's timbers.[21]

An ever-increasing call for woodworking craftsmen—carpenters, housewrights, joiners, wheelwrights, blockmakers, and ship carpenters—developed when reconstruction began after the Indian War. Gregory Dexter was one of many who fled from Providence to Aquidneck during the troubles, and in a deed of gift in 1678, made after his return, he explained that his son John had built a small cottage for him and was, at that time, also preparing another, bigger building and would erect it "in the place of o[u]r old ruines, o[u]r housing being all burnt by the enemy." The average yeoman farmer, however, was not trained or equipped for the hewing and proper framing of timbers for a well-constructed house; he and his sons could do little more than provide the rough labor. Carpenters and housewrights, who became a peripatetic lot, had to be hired for each job. Similarly, only a mason possessed the know-how to lay up a solid foundation for a house, if it were of any size, or to build a chimney with a good draft. William Corey, a Portsmouth carpenter, leased his house and thirty-eight acres of land in 1668 to John Pearce, a mason, for seven years. In part payment for the rent, the mason promised to "underpine . . . the dwelling-house with Stone and morter."[22]

21. Nathaniel B. Shurtleff and David Pulsifer, eds., *Records of the Colony of New Plymouth in New England* (Boston, 1855–61), III, 218; IV, 56–57, 66; *Providence Recs.*, IV, 6; VI, 74; XV, 189, 209, 212; XVII, 14, 119; Agreement of John and Rebecca Whipple, January 7, 1683/4 (R.I. MSS, John Hay Library, Brown University), I [oversize]; Oliver P. Fuller, *History of Warwick, Rhode Island* (Providence, 1875), 93; Francis Baylies, *An Historical Memoir of the Colony of New Plymouth*, ed. Samuel G. Drake (Boston, 1830), II, 95; *Portsmouth Recs.*, 10, 100, 136, 181.

22. The Colony of Rhode Island was beholden to Sir Edmund Andros for authorizing two courthouses in 1687: one for Newport, the other for Rochester (Kingston). Clapboards, stone, 5,000 tenpenny nails, 3,200 feet of boards, and many other materials went into the construction of the frame

Of those craftsmen working with wood, none were more important to the merchants and mariners than coopers, who fabricated all of the containers in which local products were packed for shipments to distant markets. Using staves of white or red oak, often rived from boults by farmers during the winter months, skilled coopers manufactured all sizes and kinds of casks, as containers were known generically. They made "wet cask" of white oak: barrels and half barrels, puncheons, tierces, hogsheads for ship's drinking water, for molasses, salted meats, fish, cider, beer, and oil; and "dry cask" of red oak (which was more porous than white oak) for unground corn or corn meal, peas, flour, apples, onions, ship's "Bisket" (or bread), skins, hides, tar, and miscellaneous items. Hog's fat (lard), butter, and cheese went into small firkins, soap and candles into boxes, chests, or half barrels. The coopers also fashioned barrels and larger puncheons for rum, quarter casks for brandy, and rundlets, kegs, butts, or pipes for wine, and sugar hogsheads and shooks for the Caribbean planters. For housewives they supplied dozens of articles, especially milk pails, butter churns, piggins, and the like. Inevitably some of these craftsmen grew prosperous, a few of them actually affluent. In 1655 Thomas Valestone, already the owner of a house and lot in Newport, purchased ten more acres of ground from William Coddington, and in 1693 another cooper, William Heffernan, sold off three hundred acres that he owned in the Pettaquamscutt Purchase.[23]

---

building that Thomas Starr superintended. When the General Assembly hired ten more carpenters in 1690 to complete "the Town House," the men, their beer, and rum were paid for, in part, out of the proceeds from the wool recently accepted by the treasurer for taxes. *R.I. Col. Recs.*, III, 229, 237, 262, 273; General Treasurer's Accounts, 1672–1711 (MS, R.I. Archives), 75, 84; Easton, in *R.I. Land Evidences*, I, 119; R.I. Colony Records, 1686–1715 (MS, R.I. Archives), III, May 30, 1690; Dexter, in RIHS, MSS, Misc. MSS, D-525, I; *Portsmouth Recs.*, 441; "Travel Diary of Dr. Benjamin Bullivant" [1697], in *New-York Historical Society Quarterly*, XL, 58.

23. For "Iron-bound hhds" (hogsheads), see Richardson, Account Book, Oct. 22, 1669. Nearly every craftsman listed in Appendix IV got his name

More and more well-trained artisans were employed to handle the large Rhode Island wool clip. Every year the colony produced enough wool to clothe the entire population, as well as an even larger quantity for export to other colonies. In August all sheep had to be washed thoroughly before the shearing began, and then the fleeces had to be wound (wrapped or folded up) and prepared for storage in a warehouse to await shipment or for spinning into yarn by the housewives of country and town. At both Newport and Providence there could be found numerous proficient weavers to process the yarn brought to them. In the latter community an unnamed resident's memorandum on a small piece of paper reads: "reckoned with William Austin, in June 1674. . . . To weaving of 3 yards and half of Cloath—00.02.03." Austin also dyed woolen, cotton, and flax yarns for threepence a pound. Just a month after this, little Moses Lippitt, aged six, with the consent of his parents, apprenticed himself to William Austin for fifteen and a half years to learn the trade of a weaver.[24]

In this memorandum is recorded a payment of seven pounds of "cotton wooll" by Shadrach Manton "for making stairs" at his house. Long-staple Barbados cotton was increasingly being mixed with wool to make a lighter-weight cloth for summer wear. William Harris pointed this out as early as 1674: "As to Cloath, There are made there Linsey Woollseys, and others of Cotton and Wooll, and some all Sheeps-Wool, but the better sort of Linnen is brought from England. They have many Wool combers, Spin

into the records because he owned, leased, or sold land. For instances of this, see *R.I. Land Evidences*, I, 20, 25, 62b, 113, 120, 319, 253–57, 423, 492, 557, 610.

24. Many canvas and burlap bags were needed for packing commodities, particularly wool, for shipping. In 1683 five bags of Rhode Island wool weighed 670 pounds, or 134 pounds per bag. *Sanford Letter Book*, 31; RIHS, MSS, I, 22, 24; John O. Austin, *Genealogical Dictionary of Rhode Island* (Albany, 1887), 337; Peter G. Bowden discusses shearing in *The Wool Trade in Tudor and Stuart England* (London, 1962), 23–25; *RIHS Colls.*, XXIV, 83.

their Wool very fine, of which make some Tammyes, but for their own private use."[25]

Reference has been made previously to the widespread use of leather in the seventeenth century, which gave ample work to specialized artisans. Apparently, however, after pig and sheep skins, and cow hides, had been tanned and dressed, a large proportion of them was shipped away to be manufactured elsewhere. Tanners, stampers, and leather dressers also processed quantities of deer and moose skins for the English market. They were turning out so much of this work by 1666 that, to protect graziers from thefts of their livestock, the General Assembly ordered that no person might buy, sell, exchange, or barter any hide, sheepskin, or fell (a skin with the wool still on) or have in his custody any hide or skin without its ears to prove his ownership.[26]

For local domestic use, as well as for export, the milling of corn became an important adjunct to farming. A water-powered mill was operating at Portsmouth in 1638, and a decade later two mills were grinding corn at Newport. As far as the records show, William Corey erected the first windmill on Briggs's Hill in Portsmouth in 1665, and before 1683, another water mill was established in the town. For many years before this last date, John Smith had been grinding meal for the people of Providence at his "Corne mill with the house over it."[27]

Although the colony produced no iron of its own before 1672, a supply ample enough for local needs and a small amount for

25. A *tammy* is a fine worsted cloth of a good quality, often with a glazed finish. *Oxford English Dictionary*. RIHS, MSS, I, 22; Harris, in *RIHS Colls.*, X, 147.

26. Henry W. Dorr, "The Planting and Growth of Providence," *Rhode Island Historical Tract, No. 15* (Providence, 1882), 50; *Portsmouth Recs.*, 154; *R.I. Col. Recs.*, II, 173.

27. *R.I. Col. Recs.*, I, 59, 62; R.I. Land Evidences, I, 77a, 78; *Portsmouth Recs.*, 128, 140, 216.

export became available from Plymouth Colony after 1656. The Taunton Town Meeting, fully aware of the fact that its community was within the trading domain of Rhode Island and Providence Plantations, in 1652 invited James and Henry Leonard and Ralph Russell to come there from Braintree and, with the assistance of several of the townsmen, to "set up a Bloomery Work on the Two Mile River" that was known as the Raynham Forge. Not until 1656 did work actually begin, and Samuel Maverick described the undertaking in 1660 as "a very small Iron-worke." The largest share of the bar iron made at this forge went by boat down the Taunton River to Newport and thence in ships to distant markets. The forge had two hearths in 1686 and turned out twenty to thirty tons of bar iron annually. James Leonard opened a one-hearth bloomery on Mill River in 1666, which was called the Whittenden Forge, and added another hearth there in 1693. An ingenious man who had also worked at Hammersmith in Saugus, Joseph Jenckes, operated a forge, as well as the sawmill, on the Seekonk below Pawtucket Falls on a sixty-acre tract he had acquired from the town of Providence. Both establishments were destroyed in the war years; the sawmill was rebuilt and running again within a few years, but as late as January 1684, Jenckes was petitioning the Providence Town Meeting for aid "for Rebuilding of my Iyorn workes." We know only that it was again producing bar iron sometime before 1688.[28]

Unlike other colonies, where a shortage and the high cost of

28. Evidence of the close relations of Taunton with Aquidneck is found in an agreement of July 5, 1680, in which Samuel Shiverick of Taunton, an ironworker, cleared his former partner of all debts and engaged to deliver "two hundred [pounds] of Iron and . . . one great Vice [and] . . . his working tooles" to John Reckes at Newport. *R.I. Land Evidences,* I, 152. Perez Fobes, in *MHS Colls.,* III, 170–71; J. W. D. Hall, "Ancient Iron Works at Taunton," in Old Colony Historical Society, *Collections* (1885), no. 3, pp. 131–38; *Plymouth Col. Recs.,* III, 176; IV, 98; *Providence Recs.,* IV, 6; XVII, 14; Edward N. Hartley, *Ironworks on the Saugus* (Norman, Okla., 1957), 303–4.

English iron hampered development, it appears that from 1656 the smiths and ironworkers of Newport and Providence never failed to obtain an adequate supply of bar iron, and at acceptable prices, from Taunton and, in the eighties, from the Jenckes Forge at the falls. They were accordingly able to hammer out or forge most of the simple tools used by the local farmers, chains for hauling logs, ox-plows, and carts, or for oaken buckets that hung in the wells, and also barrel hoops, locks, latches, and other ironwork for the new houses. Besides these, they manufactured small anchors, bolts, and a variety of metal fittings for the shipyards—where workers used more iron in their vessels than did the shipbuilders of contemporary England.[29]

The very insular nature of the communities on Narragansett Bay dictated that shipbuilding would be one of the first industries attempted by the settlers. At Portsmouth in February 1638/9, a "workman" was building "a Bote" for William Aspinwall, one of the banished men from Boston; the next year this shallop was seized for debt. And sometime between 1650 and 1660, Zachariah Eddy was bound apprentice to John Brown, shipwright of Rehoboth. Open shallops and pinnaces, and barques of small tonnage were regularly constructed for use on the bay and in the rivers draining into it; and throughout the whole period, ship carpenters seldom lacked commissions to make many kinds of small craft, together with ferryboats and lighters needed for special purposes. Peleg Sanford was writing to his brother William at Bridgetown, Barbados, in 1668: "Broth[e]r heare is now a shipp of about 120 tunns abuilding, and if yo please yo may have a part of her, Either an ⅛ or 1/16 or more. . . . I have not yeet taken any part of her, Neither shall I untill I heare from you." Obviously William Harris intended to include his own colony when, in a report of 1675, he

29. For the types and variety of ironware and objects used on a farm, see the inventory of William Carpenter of Pawtuxet, 1685. *Providence Recs.*, II, 35; Howard I. Chapelle, *The Search for Speed Under Sail* (New York, 1967), 14.

stated that the prime industry of New England was shipbuilding.[30]

The marked spurt in the volume of coastal and distant commerce following the Restoration and the granting of the Charter of 1663 stimulated the business of refitting and repairing visiting vessels. A prime example is the case of the *Black Horse*, a great English ship of 400 tons burthen. Having lost a mast when he was only 450 miles from Barbados in February 1662 and finding the wind against him, Captain Alexander brought the ship back to his starting point at Newport. "We worked day and night on a new mast which we finished in four days, during which time we provided ourselves with water . . . and other necessities," noted the ship's doctor. The fact that an unshaped, unstepped mast of the great size needed was immediately available points to the construction of unusually large ships at this early date.[31]

For three adventurers of New London, Joseph Wells of Westerly inaugurated shipbuilding on the Pawcatuck in 1681 by constructing *Alexander and Martha* for £165, one-eighth of the cost of building her, of which £16 was to be paid in silver and the remainder in goods. This vessel was forty feet in length by sixteen in beam, with a cabin and cookroom in the forecastle. The decked vessels commonly used in the coastal and Caribbean traffic after the mid-century were barques and ketches. The ketch was a double-ended,

30. *Aspinwall Recs.*, iii; Thomas Weston, *History of Middleboro, Massachusetts* (Boston, 1906), 43; *R.I. Col. Recs.*, I, 66, 69; *Sanford Letter Book*, 70 (where doubt is cast upon the report of 1680: "That wee have no shipping belonginge to our Colloney but only a few sloopes."); Stevens, Transcripts, I, no. 154. Often ships were built on the strand along a seashore near the source of ship's timbers. The *Fort Albany* was built for Frederick Phillipse and other Dutch merchants of New York in Barnstable County, probably on the south side of Cape Cod in 1669 (just possibly by Nicholas Davis, the Quaker of Hyannis). *Calendar of State Papers, Colonial: America and West Indies, 1669–1674*, pp. 10–11; Samuel G. Arnold, *History of the State of Rhode Island and Providence Plantations* (New York, 1859), I, 490; Appendix, IV; *RIHS Colls.*, X, 127–28.

31. Spörri, in *NEQ*, X, 545.

relatively beamy, single-decked fore-and-aft rigged vessel for coastal shipping and offshore fishing. It took its name from the hull, not, as in today's nomenclature, from the rig. Barques ranged from 30 to 50 tons burthen, ketches ran only from 16 to 30. During the last quarter of the century, the sloop, which averaged from 50 to 60 feet in length, came into popular favor with Rhode Island skippers and shippers, and by 1690 had begun to displace most other types of small vessels. "Wee have agreed with a Ship Carpenter to buyld you a slope, if you deseyer it," Richard Smith at Wickford advised Fitz-John Winthrop of New London in 1682. "The plaink is saweing, butt no demenshions agreed one; pray to send your certayne mind aboutt it, and howe shee shall be bulte and what demenshions, howe bige and what formen. Doe it as spedaly as you Can; one halfe must be money, the other goods att money prise. If you licke of it he shall procede, otherwise not. . . ." Suggestive of Quaker influence on all aspects of the economy is the casual reference of Andrew Dury of Barbados in a letter to William Penn's agent in Pennsylvania in 1687: he hoped that James Harrison would settle his balance promptly "in order to help pay for a small vessel I am building in Roades Island."[32]

After King Philip's War ended, the heavily wooded lands east and south of Rehoboth in the present towns of Somerset and Bristol were opened for lumbering. On August 18, 1687, Sir Edmund Andros authorized a grant of about two hundred acres of land "on a certain necke . . . called Shawomett [Somerset, in Massachu-

32. At Newport Roger Baster worked as a blockmaker in 1671, and Thomas Tailor operated a ropewalk there in 1676. Appendix IV. Frederick Denison, *Westerly and Its Witnesses* (Providence, 1878), 57; William A. Baker, *Colonial Vessels: Some Seventeenth-Century Sailing Craft* (Barre, Mass., 1937), 111, *et passim;* Andrew Dury to James Harrison at Pennsbury, September 1, 1687 (MS. U 1.14, Boston Public Library), I, no. 10; Letter of Richard Smith to Fitz-John Winthrop, Jr., May 12, 1682, Winthrop MSS (MHS), unclassified box, 1679–86.

setts] . . . on the westside of Taunton River" to Ralph Chapman of Newport in Road Island, Shipwright, [who] hath for the Conveniency of ships and other Vessells" prayed for a warrant to some unoccupied timberland. (See endpapers.)[33]

The most ambitious shipbuilding undertaking in the region of Narragansett Bay and the first on "Taunton Great River" was started between 1694 and 1697 by Thomas Coram, afterward a London merchant, philanthropist, and trustee of Georgia. As he recalled many years later, he was encouraged to attempt the enterprise by "the convenian[c]y of the vast great planke of oak and fir timber, and iron oar which I found abounding at a place call'd Taunton, on a navigable river about 50 miles south of Boston, but much more by water." He took English shipwrights from the Bay Town to open the yard at what is now South Dighton. The first vessel that he built, probably a ketch, was of 40 tons; and all of the bolts, spikes, and nails that went into it were forged from Raynham iron by the "engenious" Robert Crossman of Taunton. The community also produced suitable hemp and flax for making cordage and sails, which otherwise would have had to come over from England. In a complaint to the General Court of Massachusetts on March 5, 1700/1, Coram said that he had a ship of 234 tons on the stocks worth £1,000, and a second near 130 tons finished and rigged. "My Building yard which is a Large Duble sawpitt, covered with a House to worke in all weathers and [has] a new Dwelling house." The channel of the Taunton River before his yard, he insisted, was deep enough to launch a fourth-rate frigate. Previous assertions to the contrary notwithstanding, it should be abundantly evident that in the last decade of the seventeenth century all of the conditions and materials for the construction of vessels of almost any size and type were present, and the most complicated kind of industrial enterprise for that age was expand-

33. *CSM Pubs.*, XXI, 301.

ing rapidly in Rhode Island and its environs in response to the need for ever more cargo space for carrying the surplus produce of the region to far-off markets.[34]

As soon as the men of Rhode Island began to raise a surplus of livestock, they encountered perplexing problems in getting the produce to profitable and not-too-distant markets. Their water-borne trade with both Manhattan and the Bay Colony before 1647 has been treated in Chapter II. From then until the conquest of New Netherland in 1664, strained relations affected adversely all traffic along Long Island Sound. As far as commerce to the east-ward was concerned, the long voyage out and around Nantucket Island to avoid the navigational hazards of Vineyard and Nantucket sounds, as well as the treacherous shoals off Monomoy Point and Pollock Rip, was both time-consuming and perilous for such small open-decked or single-decked vessels as shallops, pinnaces, and sloops freighted with frightened and usually seasick beasts. Very soon, therefore, efforts were made to open a safer and quicker route overland to Boston.

The first step had to be the establishing of a connection between Rhode Island and the neighboring mainland of Plymouth Colony. This was accomplished in 1640 when the town meeting at Ports-mouth chose Thomas Gorton to set up a ferry at the narrowest part of the Sakonnet River, where the old Stone Bridge crossed from the island to the present Tiverton. He could charge 6d. for every person and 4d. for each goat or hog that he carried across the stream in a boat he had built for that purpose. Seven years later the town council, recognizing that traffic had increased, or-dered the new ferryman, John Sanford, to provide within fifteen days a boat capable of carrying cattle; the council also fixed new

34. *Calendar of State Papers, Colonial, 1731*, p. 58; Old Colony Historical Society, *Collections*, no. 2, pp. 29–31; Massachusetts Archives, Judicial (State House, Boston), XL, 649–50; Carl Bridenbaugh, *The Colonial Craftsman* (New York, 1950), 92.

rates: for every horse and great beast, 8*d*., and for each sheep, goat, pig, and calf, 2*d*. To ensure that no stolen animals crossed on the ferryboat, the town meeting provided in 1648 for the appointment each year of two men to inspect all cattle sold on the island before they could be shipped off; within three years it became necessary to appoint an additional two viewers besides those stationed at the ferry. The emergence of rustlers so early is indisputable proof of the rapid growth of livestock on Rhode Island.[35]

Portsmouth Ferry had more and more business each year. Richard Bulger received a license in 1654 to sell victuals, beer, and strong liquors "to Strangers that passe the ferrie, or to any persons that shall bee employed about the transportation of Cattell or travelers that are passing to and from the Iland." Soon more stringent measures were passed to regulate the ferrying of animals across the Sakonnet River, for more beasts were carried than people. The town meeting appointed four men in 1656 to take down the names of persons carrying cattle to the mainland, the date, and number of cattle, with their earmarks; they were authorized to deny passage for any cattle lacking earmarks until an acceptable explanation was offered. The same four men also watched over the loading of the cattle, even reinspecting the livestock on the boats if the loading took place at night. The extraordinarily large fine of £10 levied on anybody failing to observe these rules, plus the "further sensuer of the towne," clearly implies the existence of a perennial problem. In 1680 the number of surveyors was raised to six. Further orders governing animals taken across the river or up Mount Hope Bay into the Taunton River in private boats completed the regulation of the traffic and of the ferry, in which were carried many hundreds of livestock driven there along the "Nuport path," as well as from Portsmouth itself.

Within a year or so after the granting of the charter by King Charles II to Rhode Island and Providence Plantations, a second

35. *Portsmouth Recs.*, 15–16, 34, 38, 50.

ferry was opened at India Point, Providence. Ferries began operating from Bristol to Portsmouth and from Rehoboth to Lonsdale (Pawtucket) before 1675; at the Narrow Passage (Red Bridge) between Rehoboth and Providence in 1679; and at the Warren River crossing in Swansea in 1681/2. Caleb Carr's ferry running between Newport and Conanicut started shortly after 1676 and was the first one to connect two of the largest islands. For these insular and bayside settlements, the erection of ferries tied in with the beginnings of the highways, which eventually would link them with communities in neighboring colonies.[36]

In all probability from the time of establishing of the Portsmouth Ferry, and certainly by 1647, some kind of an Indian path ran along the east side of Mount Hope Bay up over Pocasset Hill (Fall River) and on to Taunton twenty miles away; and a road, fit at least for horse and rider, had replaced it before 1660, for in that year Portsmouth provided William Baulstone with a horse for his journey to Taunton, where he was to meet with the Plymouth commissioners. From Taunton a road led eastward to Plymouth and Sandwich, and westward through Rehoboth and onward to the ferry over the Seekonk at the Narrow Passage to Providence.[37]

The principal highroad of New England, later known as the Post Road, ran from Boston southward and westward to Manhattan Island. In 1648, however, it was but an Indian trail leading diagonally across Rhode Island. Roger Williams notified John Winthrop, Jr., at Pequot (New London) that his man William Peacock had had a very difficult time driving Joseph Wild's [Wise's] cattle from Winthrop's to Boston. Somewhere along the Pequot Path the cattle had become scattered, and the poor drover had spent six or seven

36. *Portsmouth Recs.*, 63, 73, 76, 86, 160, 167, 193, 196, 200, 205; Anna and Charles V. Chapin, *History of Rhode Island Ferries, 1640–1923* (Providence, 1925; typed copy with references in RIHS), 4–30, 227–28.

37. A highway from Taunton by way of the present Fall River was laid out to Little Compton (then in Plymouth) in 1680. Chapin, *Ferries*, 47; *Portsmouth Recs.*, 33, 34, 92.

days searching for them before he reached Cocumscussoc. Three of the four deemed lost later turned up. To Wise, the Roxbury butcher, Williams wrote that one man alone could not drive cattle amongst the barbarians, particularly without an Indian guide. From Providence to Boston the going was better, apparently, for the year following, William Arnold was procuring goods from the Bay "by his Cart." One of the strange sights along this road in 1660 was a man from Rehoboth with a broken leg being carried in a horse litter from there to Boston in February.[38]

Perhaps the most striking testimony to the importance of this highway comes from a letter of August 19, 1669, from Roger Williams to John Winthrop, Jr., who was at that time staying at Major Leverett's house in Boston: "Sir, I have encouraged Mr. [Gregory] Dexter to send you a limestone, and to salute you with this enclosed. . . . If there be any occasion of yourself (or others) to use any of this stone, Mr. Dexter hath a lusty team and lusty sons, and [a] very willing heart, (being a sanguine cheerful man) to do yourself or any (at your word especially) service. . . ." This limestone had been dug up at "Dexter's Lime Rocks" on Hackleton's Rock between the Moshassuck and Blackstone rivers in the present Lincoln. The lime for mixing mortar for use in constructing chimneys and the stone-end houses of Providence Plantations came from the limestone burned in a kiln on the premises. Massachusetts had no limestone at all before 1697, and artisans had either to use inferior lime made from oyster shells or import it by water. Just how soon the Dexter limestone began to be hauled in carts to Boston is now uncertain, but by the early eighteenth century (and for nearly two hundred years) it was a common occurrence on the Post Road.[39]

38. *Winthrop Papers*, V, 279–80, 341; *Narr. Club Pubs.*, VI, 309.

39. Sir Robert Carr and Samuel Maverick reported on Rhode Island to Lord Arlington in 1665: "Here only yet is Limestone found" in all New England. Stevens, Transcripts, I, no. 63; *Narr. Club Pubs.*, VI, 332; *Providence Recs.*, III, 66, 228–29, 241; Bradford Swan, *Gregory Dexter of London*

As new settlements were established, more roads became imperative. Ten years after the Pettaquamscutt Purchase of 1658, a road was cut from New London to Westerly to connect with the Pequot Trail. The authorities of Providence notified those of Rehoboth in 1684 that, considering "the necessity of a Road through the Countrey for Travellers to passe," they had "Erected and Stated" a way from their town over the Pawtucket (Blackstone) River along "the Westerne Plaine." The Pequot Trail, through these connecting roads, had become a highway passable (though rough) for horses, carts, and droves of animals. It ran from Westerly through Tower Hill and Pawtuxet and over Weybosset Bridge (1660, 1672) into Providence, and then forward over the bridge spanning the Blackstone at Pawtucket to "Woodcock's" (Attleboro), Wrentham, Medfield, Dedham, and Boston. We are fortunate to have accounts of journeys made from Boston to New York by John Usher, Jr., Governor Sir Edmund Andros, and an unnamed Huguenot in 1687, and by Cuthbert Potter of Virginia in 1690; there is also a description of the route printed by John Tully in *An Almanack for the Year of Our Lord MDCXCVIII*. All of them indicate the greatly increased number of travelers up and down the shore line at the close of the period. The truth is that there had always been much more going and coming in early America than the chroniclers have conceded.[40]

---

and New England (Providence, 1949), 102; Joshua Coffin, *Sketch of the History of Newbury, Newburyport, and West Newbury* (Boston, 1845), 164–65.

40. Copious documentation of the amount of travel in the colonies may be found in Carlos R. Allen, Travel and Communication in the Early Colonial Period, 1607–1720 (Ph.D. thesis, University of California, Berkeley, 1956). William D. Miller, "Ancient Paths of Pequot," in *RIHS Colls.*, XXX, 37–48, and map on cover by Norman S. Isham; Denison, *Westerly and Its Witnesses,* 57; *Providence Recs.*, II, 24; XVII, 39–40; *MHS Colls.*, 4th ser., VI, 290; Irving B. Richman, *Rhode Island: Its Making and Its Meaning* (New York, 1902), 414; William B. Weeden, *Early Rhode Island* (New York, 1910), 77, 88; *R.I. Col. Recs.*, I, 430; *CSM Pubs.*, XIII, 220; XIX, 28–32; XX, 271–78;

The cutting of roads from Portsmouth and Providence to Taun-
ton and Rehoboth served to spread the grazing economy of Rhode
Island into adjacent areas of Massachusetts and Plymouth colonies,
besides improving intercolonial communications. The inhabitants
of Rehoboth voted in July 1649 that a search should be made to
determine the nearest and most convenient way between their
town and Dedham; and they ordered in March 1655/6 that the
"new highway towards the bay shall be perfected." Not far from
Providence, east of the Seekonk River, lay Rehoboth, which Samuel
Maverick pictured in 1660 as "a Towne not despicable. It is not
above 40 Miles from Boston, betweene which there is a Comone
trade, carrying and recarrying goods by Land in Cart and on
Horseback, and they have a very fayre conveyance of goods by
water also"—that is, from Newport, the Narragansett shore, and
the islands via the Warren and Palmer rivers, and from Providence
across the Seekonk. About ten miles farther east of Rehoboth was
Taunton, which Maverick found to be a very pleasant village and
which had "a good conveyance to Boston by cart" over a road
about thirty-five miles long by way of Raynham, Bridgewater,
and Braintree. Located upon a river of the same name, Taunton was
also accessible to small craft as far up as Storehouse Point in the
present South Dighton.[41]

E. T. Fisher, trans., *Report of a French Protestant Refugee in Boston, 1687*
(Brooklyn, 1868), 18–19.

41. A glimpse of what the expansion of the Rhode Island agricultural
economy meant may be had from the inventory of William Salmin of
Rehoboth in 1685: he left fifty-nine sheep and lambs valued at £14, some
cows and oxen, and considerable quantities of "cloath, wooll, Flax, and
Corne" in the house and barn. Suffolk County, Mass., Probate Records
(MSS, Court House, Boston), VII, 61–63, 66. Over at Plymouth, Edward
Gray sued John Pococke of Portsmouth in 1679/80 for £16 for nonpayment
of 240 weight of "good marchantable sheeps woole" by October 1, 1677, as
agreed upon (a large order indeed). *Plymouth Col. Recs.*, VII, 222; Leonard
Bliss, *History of Rehoboth, Bristol County, Massachusetts* (Boston, 1836),
41, 45; Maverick, in *MHS Procs.*, 2d ser., I, 243–44.

At the house of John Howland on March 7, 1672/3, the Sandwich Monthly Meeting of Friends agreed "concerning the bad Places in the way to Road island that they be mended by the 10th day of this month, or in case wether should prevent, then the next following convenient opportunity: because of freinds General meeting at Sandwich soone following." The meeting assigned to five Friends the duty of overseeing the repair of the bad spots in the road, which, of course, had been an obstruction to overland trade even more than to attendance at meetings.[42]

Improvement in roads and transportation catered to the taste of the townsfolk of the burgeoning metropolis of New England for fresh meat and induced the butchers of Braintree, Dedham, and Boston to purchase many of their beasts alive at Rhode Island and then have most of them driven to Taunton or shipped to Storehouse Point, whence drovers took them forward to be slaughtered near the market. The leading butcher of Boston, Thomas Hawkins, was buying sheep under two years old in lots of fourteen or more from Thomas Brookes at Portsmouth in 1658, if not before. Portsmouth officials paid John Almy 35s. for driving cattle to Boston in 1663, and Bartholomew West, who assisted him, was given 5s.[43]

One of the most cherished of the guarantees that Dr. John Clarke procured in the Charter of 1663 bore directly upon all kinds of overland traffic, but that of the drovers in particular: ". . . it shall be lawfull to and for the inhabitants of the sayd Collony of Providence Plantations without let or molestation, *to passe and repasse with freedome into and through the rest of the English Collonies*, upon their lawfull and civill occasions, and to converse, and hold

<hr>

42. For "Travelling Friends" and Quaker merchants going to and from Newport and Cape Cod, see Society of Friends, Sandwich Monthly Meeting Minutes (RIHS), I, 2, 9, 10; *Sanford Letter Book*, 26–27; Maverick, in *MHS Procs.*, 3d ser., I, 243–45.

43. For Joseph Wise, the principal Roxbury butcher in 1648, see *Winthrop Papers*, V, 240, 264, 265; *Portsmouth Recs.*, 123, 352–53.

commerce and trade, with such of the inhabitants . . . as shall be willing to admit them thereunto, they behaving themselves peaceably among them; any act, clause, or sentence, in any of the sayd Collonies provided, or that shall bee provided, to the contrary notwithstanding. . . ." Freedom of trade was every bit as vital as freedom of conscience, and both had been equally threatened by the Rhode Islanders' jealous and fearful neighbors.[44]

After this right to economic survival was made official, animals fattened for market—hogs, sheep, cattle, and also horses—crowded the roads to the Bay more than ever. Drovers grew in importance and reliability, and were often entrusted with several sorts of commissions. Philip Jones of Newport promised Samuel Sewall of Boston to send him £4 10s. in payment for fish "by the Drover" as soon as he came to Rhode Island. From Newport, too, Peleg Sanford advised his uncle, Samuel Hutchinson of the Bay Town, in 1667 that forty or fifty sheep were needed to "incorage any [drover] to come down with them" from Aquidneck.[45]

Despite the cessation of all trips by drovers during the Indian troubles, the trips started up promptly in 1677, and within three years this inland commerce had grown so heavy that the Great and General Court was prodded into action to cut it down. Local graziers were complaining that persons from nearby colonies were driving in neat cattle, horses, and swine, "thereby filling up our markets," so that Bay-bred animals did not sell, and precious pine-tree shillings were being drained from the colony. To relieve them, the General Court laid an impost upon all beasts imported into

44. William Macdonald, ed., *Select Charters and Other Documents Illustrative of American History, 1606–1775* (New York, 1899), 132–33 (italics mine).

45. Travelers from Boston to Connecticut and New York often went overland by way of Taunton and Rehoboth to Portsmouth and Newport, and from there by water to their destinations. John Hull, Letter Book, 1670–1685 (MS, typed copy in American Antiquarian Society, Worcester), 243, 576, 636; *Sanford Letter Book*, 35–36.

Massachusetts Bay: on neat cattle 2s. 6d. a head, swine 1s., sheep 6d., and for horses 2s. 6d. The court also issued elaborate directions for collecting the duties at the border towns as the animals crossed the boundary.

This early venture in protectionism went into effect on November 20, 1680, but the next year, on May 11, the General Court saw cause to repeal it "to all intents and purposes, soe far as it relates to such as are in confederation with us." It is difficult to believe that anyone in New England was fooled by this somewhat cowardly double talk, which meant, in plain English, that only the drovers from Rhode Island would be forced to pay the impost set by a law ostensibly no longer on the books. In the light of the Rhode Island Charter of 1663, this measure seems of questionable legality, and perhaps this may explain the deviousness of the Bay authorities. Whether the impost had the desired effect before the vacating of the Massachusetts Bay Company's charter on June 21, 1684, is not now known. Certainly the men of Taunton, the border town where most of the drovers assembled and made up their herds and flocks, had no desire to encumber the brisk trade that was their main source of prosperity. Under the Dominion of New England, free trade prevailed everywhere, and gentlemen and others passing along the highroads once more encountered augmented processions of the denizens of Naboth's Meadows on their way to the butchers of the Puritan metropolis.[46]

46. New Hampshire was made a royal province in 1679 and may not have been included in the United Colonies as it was when it was a part of Massachusetts Bay. Whether its drovers were regarded as "our confoederates" by the members of the General Court cannot be determined. But their clear intent was to collect from the Rhode Islanders. William H. Whitmore, ed., *The Colonial Laws of Massachusetts. Reprinted from the Edition of 1672, with Supplements through 1686* . . . (Boston, 1887), 283, 287; Nathaniel B. Shurtleff, ed., *Records of the Governor and Company of Massachusetts Bay in New England* (Boston, 1854), V, 202–3, 209.

V

AGRICULTURE

USHERS IN

COMMERCE

FROM 1660 to 1690 the Colony of Rhode Island and Providence Plantations experienced a steady economic growth, one that was interrupted only during the two conflicts with the Dutch (1665-67, 1673-74) and King Philip's War (1675-76). The coming of the Quakers in 1657, the guarantees of security in the charter granted by King Charles II in 1663, the widening of markets to the southward and in the Caribbean, and the opening up of roads to adjacent colonies combined to stimulate already developing commercial enterprises. In short, the settlers were raising more of all kinds of livestock; growing larger crops of corn, oats, barley, and hay; and producing more marketable goods each year than they consumed or than they had means to transport. They had to find additional cargo space in both those ships owned locally and the ships of other colonies. These were the years in which the grandees of Newport benefited most of all. In 1690 they could take immense satisfaction in having created a substantial amount of wealth in cultivated lands and farm buildings, in warehouses, wharves, and ships, in vendible cargoes, in bills of exchange on London, and, in what is most surprising, small hoards of gold and silver.

Foresight and tireless energy were the hallmarks of the leading Rhode Islanders, and by the close of the period, under the pressure of the complexities of seaborne commerce, numerous stockmen could qualify as merchants also. In framing answers to queries made in 1680 by the Lords of Trade and Plantations, Governor

Peleg Sanford and the council shrewdly obfuscated the distinction: "Wee answer that wee have severall men that deale in buyinge and sellinge although they cannot properly be called Merchants . . . but the most of our Colloney live comfortably by improving the wilderness," and, moreover, "that the great obstruction concerninge trade is the want of Merchants and Men of considerable Estates amongst us." This was the truth but far from the whole truth, and many a latter-day commentator has taken it too literally. From the earliest days, the colony contained some "Men of considerable Estates," and almost forty individuals were designated "merchants" in contemporary legal documents. Like the settlers of any other colony—English, French, Dutch, or Spanish—they could have used more capital, but their one desire was always to manage this tiny agricultural-commercial experiment by themselves. It was caution based upon fear of interference or regulation from the outside that impelled these worthies to answer as they did.[1]

The assembling of cargoes for vessels, whose time of arrival was never certain, necessitated the collection in advance of barrels of meat, grain, or meal, boxes of various articles, and other things at a specified spot near the waterside. Prosperous merchants built warehouses where they stored incoming cargo or goods awaiting shipment. In July 1673, for instance, the master of the brigantine *Good Hope*, bound from New Bern in Carolina to Fowey, Cornwall, placed "Nyne Tunnes being Thirty six hogsheads of tobacco" in Caleb Carr's warehouse at Newport while the ship's protest over freight charges was being settled at Boston. Besides the storing of miscellaneous containers rolled, carried, or carted through the great door of one of these structures, much of the packing went on inside

1. In the eighteenth century, for obvious reasons, it became the settled habit of colonial officials, even of royal governors, to underestimate, often to conceal, the actual degree of development and amount of wealth in their several provinces. Stevens, Transcripts, II, no. 154; Samuel G. Arnold, *History of the State of Rhode Island and Providence Plantations* (New York, 1859), I, 49, 491; and the list of merchants in Appendix III.

the warehouses, for the perishable nature of much of the produce to be shipped and the great heat to which cargoes would be subjected in the holds of vessels voyaging to the tropics called for the labor of skilled packers. As an example, cranberries, intended for England or the West Indies, had to be packed in new, scalded casks and covered with water to avoid spoilage, though sometimes the berries arrived tasting of the wood. The majority of warehouses were not much larger than a medium-sized dwelling house or barn. Very often the merchant who owned a warehouse had a small space walled off in the corner for his counting room, where his letter books and account books were kept—unless, of course, he also owned a countinghouse close by.[2]

If a merchant possessed one or more vessels or wanted to supervise the lading and unlading of ships, he aspired to a wharf of his own and to putting up one or more warehouses on it. The first large wharf at Newport was probably erected in the late forties or fifties, though we only learn about it from a letter of Peleg Sanford in January 1666/7. Writing to his brother William at Barbados, he requested that no goods be shipped northward unless the master agreed "to put it on shoare at Father Brenton['s] wharf." That appears to have been the only large wharf for some time inasmuch as Randall Holden wrote in 1679 of arriving at Newport and being met "on *the* wharfe" by the governor and others. Shipping had increased sufficiently at the head of Narragansett Bay by 1680 that the town of Providence granted Pardon Tillinghast a small piece of ground for the erection of a storehouse and the right to put up a wharf. The next year at Portsmouth, William Earle, John Borden, Abiel Tripp, and Joseph Anthony each obtained authorization to build or to finish a wharf of his own. Newport acquired two sizable

2. Dr. John Clarke sold his warehouse to Richard Smith for £20 sterling in 1674. It had previously been owned by Francis Brinley. *R.I. Land Evidences*, I, 44; *CSM Pubs.*, XXIX, 277–85; A. Rupert Hall and Marie B. Hall, eds., *The Correspondence of Henry Oldenburg* (Madison, Wisc., 1969, 1970, 1971), VI, 395; VII, 11, 143, 202, 569; VIII, 267.

wharves in the eighties, for when Benedict Arnold, Jeremiah Bowen, Ralph Chapman, Simon Parrott, Walter Newbury, William Allen, and some others asked for permission to "build a wharf into the Sea," it was granted on "the same tearmes and conditions as the town grant for the lands where the new Long Wharf stands." No longer was it necessary to unlade most vessels into lighters as it had been in earlier years.[3]

It is difficult to be precise, but certainly as many vessels sailed with venture cargoes as with shipments on order. Arrangements for the latter entailed much correspondence, which absorbed the time of both the merchant and his apprentices, for not only did the merchants have to assume the task of collecting the cargoes of animals and goods from all over the colony, but they also had to arrange, before sending them out, for someone—the ship's captain, a supercargo, or a merchant—to sell them at the other end of the voyage. In addition to acting in his own behalf, a Rhode Island merchant often served as the agent for a distant mercantile house. The Quakers usually confined their business to other Friends: at Providence John Whipple acted for those in Boston, Bridgewater, Plymouth Colony, Rehoboth, and Newport. He bought rum through Daniel Gould on Rhode Island, and in turn looked after forwarding a trunk full of goods Edward Shippen wanted delivered to Newport. Frequently, too, a correspondent in a distant place made "my good Friend John Whipple" his "Lawfull Attorney" to collect money or goods or estates due; Stephen Paine of Rehoboth used Whipple to recover what was owed to him from the estate of Leonard Smith of Providence in 1670.[4]

3. *Sanford Letter Book*, 21; Randall Holden and John Greene to William Blathwayt, August 7, 1679, Blathwayt Papers (MS, Colonial Williamsburg, Va.), XI (italics mine); *R.I. Land Evidences*, I, 63–64; *Providence Recs.*, VIII, 62; *Portsmouth Recs.*, 217, 218; Newport Town Meeting Records (MS, NHS), April 29, 1685.

4. On some occasions, if the transactions were large, a merchant in another seaport sent a "bookkeeper" to Newport to look after his business in the

Attracted by the salubrious climate, a cultivated royalist sympathizer, Francis Brinley, moved in 1651, possibly a bit earlier, from Barbados to Rhode Island. Almost immediately he began to sign himself Recorder or notary and before long began to act as the agent for merchants and planters of Barbados. In 1671 he put his knowledge of admiralty law to work by helping the Dutch and English owners of a great ship of 500 tons wrecked on the west end of Fishers Island in 1668. When William Harris was taken at sea and made "a Captive in Turkey," he wrote home to make Brinley the agent for turning his estate over to the pirates to redeem him; his wife, Susan, designated John Whipple to act as her attorney. All this time Brinley was reaping the rewards of his investments in land: some of his clients in Essex County, Massachusetts, delivered to Joshua Buffum, a Quaker artisan of Salem, two bags of sheep wool weighing about three hundred pounds, which brought £10 8s. 9d. When the Dominion of New England was set up, Francis Brinley became chief judge and the highest ranking royal officer of the region between 1687 and 1689.[5]

One of the important and interesting, though as yet uninvestigated, features of early American law was the use of intercolonial legal processes, especially with the expansion of colonial commerce after 1660. Most of the cases involved debts, money transfers, or breaches of maritime practices under the Laws of Oléron, and the proper settlement of these disputes was fundamental to any orderly operation of trade and navigation. The concept of giving "full faith

---

countinghouse of a local merchant. Theodore Atkinson of Boston did this in 1659 when he placed Clement Salmin at Robert Moone's office in Newport. William B. Trask, ed., *Suffolk Deeds* (Boston, 1892), VI, 337; Providence Town Papers (MS, RIHS), I, 107; RIHS, MSS, I, 38, 41, 44, 58, 64; *Providence Recs.*, XIV, 78.

5. R.I. Land Evidences, I, 110–11; for Brinley's library, *New England Historical and Genealogical Register*, IX, 79; XII, 75–78; Providence Town Papers, I, 141; Joshua Buffum, Account Book, 1669–1700 (MS, Essex Institute, Salem), 113.

and credit" in one colony to the laws and judicial proceedings of another or of England developed very early in colonial practice. In Newport harbor in January 1658/9 lay *Black Bird*, a barque owned in part by George Potter of Virginia. His agent, Robert Potter, in need of money to pay for sails, cables, anchors, rigging, provisions, and seamen's wages, borrowed £168 9s. sterling of William Brenton. Robert Potter sold his kinsman's interest in the barque, together with the goods on board, to satisfy the loan on condition that George Potter would give security at Charles City County Court within two days of *Black Bird*'s arrival in the James River. In another case William Garde, a merchant of Rhode Island, brought a suit in Talbot County, Maryland, in 1669/70 to attach the estate of Richard Edge for 1,000 pounds of tobacco. After he took the oath, the court allowed him 800 pounds of tobacco as "his Just debt." Garde was back in the Talbot County Court again two months later suing for 1,315 pounds of tobacco due from Philip Lloyd, which the justices ordered this member of a distinguished family to pay, at the same time directing William Young to satisfy Garde's claim for 200 pounds of leaf and the costs of the suit.[6]

Other demands on court time arose when a vessel put into port after being buffeted in a severe storm on the Atlantic and filed a ship's protest. This was a statement sworn to (or affirmed, by Quakers) before a court by the master of a ship newly entered in a harbor that such damage as his vessel and cargo had sustained in a recent storm or other natural event had been caused by wind or wave—an act of God—and that he could not be held responsible. Samuel Andrews of the ketch *Providence* and three witnesses from his crew protested in April 1671 that, on a voyage from Providence

6. See the case of Edward Lecke, Rhode Island merchant, in Kent County Court, April 1, 1661, which was handled by a Maryland attorney. *Archives of Maryland*, ed. J. Hall Pleasants (Baltimore, 1937), LIV, 210, 211, 453, 461; Beverley W. Fleet, comp., *Virginia Colonial Abstracts* (mimeographed, Baltimore, 1961), XI, 35.

to New York, contrary winds had forced them ashore on a sandy
Rhode Island beach open to the ocean and "very great Brakers."
A few months before this incident, John Herbert of the sloop
Swan, which had run aground off Monomoy Point made "Publick-
ly . . . [a] Protest against the sea, winde, and bad wether, for all
Losses"; and the barque *Reserve* of New London, bound from
Barbados to Newport in 1689, lost all the casks from her deck in a
blow of October 9 in latitude 39° 35″ "by dead reckoning," so her
master and mate made oath.[7]

No aspect of the merchant's responsibilities demanded more
wisdom, judgment, and human understanding than his dealings
with shipowners, master mariners, and their crews. Members of
the Society of Friends preferred to traffic with other Friends be-
cause they had the weighty and reliable authority of the meeting
behind them. Men of other denominations could, in a lesser degree,
depend upon their coreligionists. Still, before the Rhode Island
Court of Trial and in the courts of other colonies came many cases
for settlement of breaches of charter party, suits for nonperformance
of bills of lading, and like matters. In the court of Charles County,
Maryland, Thomas Michele sued Daniel Hutt, master of the vessel
he had served on, for eight months' wages denied to him. Hutt
claimed that he had not hired Michele, but rather that he had been
"shipped by Mr. William Brenton of Newport in Rhode Island
Merchant." When the petitioner failed to prove the contrary, the
justices nonsuited the case. Here again in lawsuits tried outside the
home colony there is evidence of the wide range of trade operations
fanning out from Rhode Island.[8]

7. *R.I. Land Evidences*, I, 95, 101, 224.

8. An amusing instance of Quaker directness and sarcasm over accounts
is found in a letter of William Asten of May 16, 1680, RIHS, MSS, I, 48;
Helen Capewell, ed., *Records of the Court of Trials of the Colony of Prov-
idence Plantations, 1647–1670* (Providence, 1920), II, 99–100; *Archives of
Maryland*, LIII, 41–42; *R.I. Col. Recs.*, I, 314, 330.

The Antinomian leaders and their more numerous Quaker successors in the merchant class filled many town and provincial offices where they used their understanding of both agriculture and commerce to procure regulations and enactments not for their benefit alone but for the common weal. As men of unquestioned probity and virtue, they evinced (to the modern onlooker at least) an unusually high degree of public responsibility. This Quaker spirit of morality finds homely expression in the lines that Thomas Richardson inscribed in his account book in a large and clear hand in November 1668:

> Give not thy Strength to Women.
> Nor thy ways to that which destroyeth
> Kings. Nither lett pation overcome the[e],
> But let Vertue guid thee in all thy ways.[9]

When war broke out between England and Holland in 1653, the island assembly, under the aegis of William Coddington and the urging of the authorities in England, passed some vigorous measures against the Dutch. It issued privateering commissions to three local mariners and erected a court of admiralty to try prize cases. Such a procedure upset Providence and Warwick officers, who feared that all New England might be set afire. Significantly, as soon as the Dutch and English concluded peace, the colony led all others in New England in resuming traffic with Manhattan. More to the taste of the merchants was a measure of 1655 appointing two "houses of entertainment" for strangers at both Newport and Portsmouth, with the option of adding a third in either place if the number of strangers coming and going warranted it. There was an adverse side to these seeming gestures of hospitality, however, for numerous complaints came from masters of vessels from foreign ports that their seamen, who patronized the taverns, had been attached for debt and imprisoned and consequently could

9. William and Thomas Richardson, Account Book, 1662–1702 (MS, NHS), November 1668, at foot of account with William Love.

not sail. In 1679 the granting of credit to sailors on shore was prohibited.[10]

To help finance the colony's government, an excise was laid on all imported wines and spirituous liquors not the product of England or the Dominions; measures akin to this held in virtually all existing countries. In 1658 the assembly ordered each of the towns to choose two men to board vessels and search industriously for any strong waters; any liquor smuggled ashore without paying the excise was to be seized. Complaints came from Warwick in 1661 that it "suffered abues, about Excise by Reasin of licquers land-inge at Newport," and a protest was lodged with the assembly. Five years later the Warwick Town Meeting voted to have "a Constant water bayly or searchers office" set up and directed the constables to board any vessel entering any harbor within the precincts of Warwick that might be carrying dutiable liquors. Still worried about evasions of the excise, the members of the assembly set new rates on all wines and strong waters: 10s. a pipe, 20s. a tun, and so on, in minute detail. This concern indicates a mounting trade in wines and Dutch brandies, which had its origin in New Amsterdam before 1664 and then in New York, or New-foundland, and at Fayal and the other Wine Islands, often via Barbados or Curaçao.[11]

William Brenton, Dr. John Clarke, and William Baulstone knew full well that their surpluses of livestock must be sold profitably in other parts of America if they were to continue to drink fine wines and sip old Dutch brandies. They glimpsed the future possibilities of Narragansett Bay and described it flamboyantly, yet truthfully withal, to Lord Clarendon in 1665: "this Bay which in very deed is the most Excellent in New-England considering the climate, most healthfull Scite, most commodious in the midle of the

10. Arnold, *Rhode Island*, I, 246–49; *R.I. Col. Recs.*, I, 266, 270–71; III, 31–32.

11. *R.I. Col. Recs.*, I, 382; II, 352–53; Howard M. Chapin, ed., *The Early Records of the Town of Warwick* (Providence, 1926), 126, 155.

Colonies; Harbors, most safe for the biggest ship's that ever sayled the sea; and of all sorts whatever, and for outlet and inlett soe good as none can equall it, that in the hardest winters, when the Massachusetts and others, to the East and west are fast-locked up with strong doores of Ice, this is alwayes open: besides the conveniencie of the Mainland and Islands att the very entrance soe near each other." What they most ardently desired was "some act of Grace extending some Peculiar Priviledge in Point of freeness of commerce hence to others His Majesties Dominions, with some ease in some measure as to Taxes upon that [which] is Imported or Exported" for some years. Once again, in 1686, upon notifying King James II of their loyal acquiesence to incorporation in the Dominion of New England, Governor Clarke and the Council begged for a continuance of the privileges guaranteed in their vacated charter, and further requested that Newport, "forasmuch as [it] lays in the heart of all your Majestie's Collonies, . . . be made a free port for navigation and entries, paying duties"! Neither of the Stuart kings, however, was disposed to contravene mercantile opinion by suspending operation of the Acts of Trade and Navigation in any case whatsoever.[12]

Recognizing that many large ships from other ports and a growing number owned in the colony were entering and leaving Narragansett Bay every year, the General Assembly ordered in 1679 that the masters of all vessels of more than 20 tons burthen must give notice to the authorities upon entering and post a notice of intention

12. The Rhode Islanders continued to count heavily upon further royal support after Charles II granted them a charter. Another letter to Lord Clarendon in 1666 about fixing the boundary with Plymouth prayed for the land forming the eastern shore of Narragansett Bay (Tiverton and Little Compton) because some persons from Aquidneck had purchased lands there from the Indians; and the extension of Rhode Island's jurisdiction across the Sakonnet seemed necessary because of the need of settling questions of law and property that were made difficult in view of the remoteness of the district from Plymouth. *R.I Col. Recs.*, I, 165; III, 193; "Clarendon Papers," in New-York Historical Society, *Collections* (1869), 143–44.

of departure three days before leaving port. The authority referred to was merely a naval office under the direction of the provincial government, and this did not satisfy Edward Randolph, who stressed the royal orders about such arrangements. In response to his insistence, in March 1682, the governor and council ordered the creation of a naval office at Newport where the captains of all "deck vessels" had to register entries, ladings, clearances, and post bonds for the proper observing of the laws of trade. After this date, too, masters of every vessel of 40 tons or upward had to pay a fee of 5s. 6d. for each bond of entry and discharge; the fee for those under 40 tons was set at 2s. 6d. With the resumption of self-government under the charter following the Revolution of 1688, the General Assembly directed in 1690 that all ships and vessels "of what sort soever" above 10 tons from any English colony or plantation except Rhode Island should pay 1s. 10d. or one pound of powder to the deputy collector for the island's use "if they unlade or brak bulk in this harbor of Newport." Only a busy seaport much frequented by strange ships would have required such regulations.[13]

In all discussions of colonial economies, emphasis is always placed primarily upon the siphoning of specie, of gold and silver, from new settlements to pay for the manufactured goods not produced by them—and rightly so. Taken as a whole region, seventeenth-century New England offered no exception to this ancient maxim. But what of the Colony of Rhode Island and Providence Plantations? Was its economy so typical that inquiry into money problems or the balance of trade has never been deemed necessary?

At the time that the Quakers came to Newport, all the Rhode Islanders believed that their livelihood depended upon how Massachusetts—with Plymouth, Connecticut, and New Haven in train —admitted them to or denied them access to the markets of the United Colonies. They and their fellows suffered economic punish-

13. *R.I. Col. Recs.*, III, 32, 110–11, 242, 278.

ment because they would not expel all members of the Society of Friends from their bounds. One turn of Fortune's wheel might put them out of business completely.

Under the astute leadership of the Quakers and the unplanned benevolence of the royal authorities, however, the dominance of Massachusetts Bay was gradually but surely lessened. The men of Aquidneck and Providence who had agricultural produce to sell turned their faces southward and westward in a phenomenally successful search for markets. After the Dutch surrendered in 1664, the Rhode Islanders kept on pushing their trade at Manhattan with the New Yorkers with added vigor; and under Quaker auspices, a lucrative traffic with Friends settled on Chesapeake Bay and along Albemarle Sound in Carolina opened for pork, beef, corn, and horses. Again, with Quaker mariners literally at the helm, pounds, shillings, and pence clinked into the coffers of the grandees of Newport when vessels sailed back into the harbor from Barbados, Antigua, Nevis, Saint Christopher, or Jamaica. After 1680 the vast new and wealthy Quaker societies of the Jerseys and Pennsylvania welcomed all kinds of trade with the members of the New England Yearly Meeting.

Meanwhile, ever since the fifties, the demand for livestock by the butchers of Massachusetts ensured to the people of the Isle of Error an increasingly profitable overland traffic that drew off considerable sums of New England silver money, for apparently the Rhode Islanders were buying less from the Bay traders than they sold to them. By way of the monthly meetings in Plymouth Colony and the settlers at Taunton and Rehoboth, the spacious area of present southeastern Massachusetts had been drawn into the commercial orbit of Newport and Providence, and overland and water-borne trades were well managed. Actually, comparatively few "European Goods" were ever imported during this century. Only a few Rhode Island gentry ever purchased elegant clothes, finery, and silver plate, while the vast majority of the remaining population worked in leather breeches and aprons or dressed in cloth spun and woven from wool or flax of their own raising or from West Indian cotton paid for by products of the Narragansett Bay region. They needed no foreign iron, which saved them much expense, and the many craftsmen living in the colony could fabricate most of what the people needed out of locally produced wood, leather, and wool, or from Raynham iron.

A windfall of silver and gold nourished the colony's economy early in 1679 when two privateers (or pirates) concerned in several prizes taken from the Spanish in the Bay of Matanzas, contrary to their covenants to go to Boston, "in a perfidious and treacherous manner . . . divided and shared the prizes at Road Island." From Jamaica the next year, Governor Lord Carlisle informed the Lords of Trade and Plantations that privateers from his island raided the Spanish on the Gulf of Honduras, and when they returned told him plainly that if they could not trade at Port Royal, they would abandon Jamaica "and sail to Rhode Island or the Dutch," where they knew they would be "well entertained." Although these privateers were prevented from sailing northward, others did so. According to Edward Randolph in 1688: "A great Treasure is stoln ashore up and down the Country" by certain pirates, one of whose ships lay at anchor at Newport as he wrote.[14]

The unperceived miracle was that merchants and owners of large estates had prospered, and those who no longer wanted more land, or needed to rebuild ruined houses, or desired to invest in colony-built vessels and venture cargoes often turned their gains into hard money. Walter Newbury squared his account with two London merchants in 1686 with "five severall bills of Exchainge Containing £340 Starling money of England," plus "Sixty three pounds three shillings Starling . . . and ninty peces of Eight Spanish money." The total, £483 8s., was a large sum and reveals that a

14. *CSM Pubs.*, XXX, 988; *Calendar of State Papers, Colonial, 1677–1680,* p. 443; R. N. Toppan and A. T. S. Goodrick, *Edward Randolph . . . ,* Prince Society Publications (Boston, 1909), VI, 275; *New England Historical and Genealogical Register,* LXXXIII, 84.

newly arrived Quaker merchant with the proper connections in England and Barbados could do as well as any Boston merchant. Stephen Arnold of Pawtuxet left an estate in 1699 valued at £495 11s. 1d., of which £130 was in gold and silver and £146 5s. 3d. was "money due by bills."[15]

Sales of the fat mutton of Rhode Island and the salted meats of other beasts frequently brought to the humbler inhabitants that rare commodity—hard money. In 1671 Mary Deering, a widow, sold off her land on Block Island for £145 in "Silver of New England," and a shipwright of Portsmouth, Robert Hazard, paid in silver for five hundred acres of land he had bought in the King's Province. Five years after this transaction, Mathew Boomer, a Newport cordwainer, paid £45 in silver for half of lot number 4 on the east side of Taunton River and promptly sold a quarter of it to John Read, a fellow cordwainer, for £22 10s. in silver. At his death in 1687, Richard Barnes of Newport, probably a seafaring man, left a personal estate inventoried at £148 9s., which included both "cash in pocket" and "Cash found in his Chest and one Guinney."[16]

Such evidence as has survived does not permit us to demonstrate with mathematical certainty that the Colony of Rhode Island and Providence Plantations enjoyed a favorable balance of trade in 1690, but it does strongly fortify this conclusion. In its trading relations

15. A law of May 1, 1678, to guarantee creditors payment from bankrupts in proportion to the assets remaining and appointing such men as Peleg Sanford, John Cranston, and John Coggeshall as commissioners was repealed on June 12, 1678, without explanation. It may indicate that the growth of population and wealth was sufficient to warrant such action. *R.I. Col. Recs.*, II, 7–8, 10; "The Walter Newbury Shipping Book," in *RIHS Colls.*, XXIV, 88–89; William B. Weeden, *Early Rhode Island* (New York, 1910), 120–21.

16. Suffolk County, Mass., Probate Records (MSS, Court House, Boston), VI, 46; Horace E. Turner, comp., Colonial Land Evidences (Rhode Island) [MS, NHS], bk. I, 4, 5, 45, 83, 136, 169, *et passim* reveal a surprising amount of Massachusetts silver and Spanish pieces of eight in the inventories of ordinary Rhode Islanders.

with Massachusetts, the tiny colony appears to have had the advantage; certainly the merchants and stockmen of the Bay Colony attested bitterly to the loss of coin to their despised neighbors. Nor is it likely that Rhode Island shippers trafficked to their disadvantage in the Caribbean or elsewhere along the Atlantic perimeter. They had turned to the sea for outlets, and not only had they found them, but, through Quaker enterprise and ingenuity, they had established a substantial water-borne commerce that enabled them to traffic free, for the most part, from the overlordship of the Bostoners. Who can deny that they had achieved success in agriculture and trade?

THE ocean lanes leading from Narragansett Bay to English and foreign Atlantic markets had been explored, at least were fairly well known, before the coming of the Quakers in 1657. The contribution of the Friends was to extend and exploit these routes by sending out and receiving a larger volume of traffic each year. In a surprisingly short time, they expanded and rationalized the commerce of Rhode Island and its environs with notable success. Vessels came and went up and down the eastern coast of North America and to the Caribbean, or they crossed the sea to the British Isles, continental Europe, and the Wine Islands—even to West Africa. Trade flowed along all of these avenues simultaneously, of course, and frequently in the same ship.

The unrelenting hostility of the Puritan leaders at the Bay towards the Quakers before the Crown started to restrain them profoundly affected the course of trade along the New England coast. North of Boston, the only monthly meetings of the Friends were at Salem and Piscataqua, and both of these regions were under the commercial suzerainty of the Massachusetts traders; but from Duxbury around Cape Cod and southward and westward to Oyster Bay, save in Connecticut, was Quaker territory, which their merchants had made an almost private preserve. The account book of William and Thomas Richardson covering the years 1662 to 1668 contains fragments of the story of this spreading of trade far beyond normal expectancy through Friendly channels.

A chance occurrence gave the Quakers the entry into the commercial circle at Boston. Edward Shippen, nurtured as an Anglican in Yorkshire, came to Boston in 1668 and there, possessed of a small fund of capital, proceeded to make a fortune and acquire sizable investments in land. Convinced of the "Truth" about 1671, he thenceforth suffered frequent harassments for his faith but, at the same time, made himself the principal mercantile figure among the Friends of New England, even surpassing Nicholas Shapleigh of Kittery as a trader. At the Yearly Meeting held at Newport in 1686, Shippen agreed to look after the welfare of all traveling Friends who went to Boston. Then in 1688 he moved to Newport and, eventually, to the great Quaker entrepôt of Philadelphia, where he earned great prominence and occupied numerous political offices.[17]

Acceptance by the most influential merchants was the chief reason Edward Shippen managed to prosper at Boston despite his religious views. He joined with John Saffin, John Usher, James Whetcombe, and Andrew Belcher in 1680 in sending the ship *Elizabeth* under William Warren "for Guinea." This slaving voyage, as it developed, involved the promoters in a series of shady maneuvers in which the authorities of Rhode Island come off much better morally than their counterparts of Massachusetts Bay.

The original instructions to the master were that he was to put in at Swansea on his return, but on June 12 of the following year, the partners wrote to Warren advising him that, having heard that "the Governor of Rhode Island Understanding, doth . . . intend to Ceise you," they were sending new orders by the bearer, William Welstead. He was not to go to Swansea but to go directly to Nantasket; and there, if not before, he was to deliver the Negroes to Welstead. The next evening he was to go into Boston and if asked

17. Society of Friends [New England], The Yearly Meeting Book, 1683 (MS, RIHS), 1–3.

"what place from whence" he came, to answer "from Martin's Vinyard" or any other place he thought fit. To Welstead, the partners gave written instructions directing him to proceed to Rhode Island with all dispatch and take a position off Castle Hill at the entrance to Narragansett Bay and intercept Warren and deliver their letter. He was to sail at once, with Warren, for Nantasket and after taking on such Negroes as were on board *Elizabeth*, to go by night to Boston, where the slaves could be landed. The final admonition of his principals has more of a Puritan than a Quaker flavor: "Keep your men [in your boat] Ignorant of your designe and *Improve your time what you can in fishing* or else what you can to defray our charges, but not prejudicial to our mane designe...."[18]

Under the aegis of Edward Shippen, trade with the Bay Town increased, though it never became large in proportion to the total commerce of the colony. It came about as the people of Rhode Island and Providence Plantations grew more affluent, a condition so evident in the eighties. Demands for larger importation of manufactured and other European goods from Boston mounted, and it appears to have been largely carried on by Quaker merchants in Quaker vessels. Benjamin Newbury, for instance, ordered and received in 1685 from Boston in the sloop *Exchange*, Jonathan Parker master, a sizable shipment from Edward Shippen, Nathaniel Byfield, Anthony Stoddard, and a merchant named Taylor; it consisted of nails, starch, tinware, Smyrna raisins, dry goods, scythes, and a barrel of rum. An "Accot of things Bought at Boston" by Benjamin Newbury in 1685 or 1686 lists Latin textbooks, Lockyer's Pills, 2 gross of horn rings, 2½ dozen "Pasteboard boxes," assorted drugs, "Toys," ship's rigging, and surgical instruments—European goods all. Noticeably missing were woolen cloth, clothing, and

18. Letters to William Warren and William Welstead, June 12, 1681, in Jeffries Family Papers (MS, MHS), II, 149; for Andrew Belcher's Accounts for Negroes, September 21, 1681, Miscellaneous Bound Manuscripts (MHS), 1679–1687.

iron. Trade also went in the opposite direction, from Newport to Boston. In 1686 Walter Newbury, a Friend recently come over from London, forwarded to Edward Shippen 6½ tons of "brazalette wood," a bundle of deerskins and beaver pelts, 7 bags of sheep's wool, and 4 hogsheads of sugar; he also shipped 19½ barrels of flour (probably collected on Long Island or in Connecticut) for Elizabeth Perry, a Quakeress. In 1687 Shippen sent payments totaling £41 5s. to five Newport merchants in care of Benjamin Newbury.[19]

One may trace in the well-known *Letter Book of Peleg Sanford, 1666–1668* the commercial and agricultural transactions among the Hutchinsons and Sanfords of Newport and Boston and branches in Portsmouth, and also with members of the tribe in Barbados and London. Kinship had always proved rather stronger than religious affiliations among them, and these close family ties prevailed in business, furthered by frequent intermarriages, throughout the colonial era. They enjoyed a strategic set of locations for a classic medieval family business; there was nothing peculiarly Puritan or American about it. Peleg Sanford imported cutlery, large quantities of nails of all sizes, canvas, several kinds of cloth, and gunpowder from England by way of the Hutchinson uncles at Boston, through whom he also procured some of John Hull's silver plate and small articles of brazier's ware. But it must be stressed that, like those of most Newporters, Sanford's purchases of manufactured goods were ordinarily small orders, even when he planned to sell them by retail at his shop in Newport or at Taunton through his Brenton relatives. His principal trade was the exchange with his brother William at Bridgetown of Rhode Island livestock and produce for the cotton, rum, molasses, and sugar of Barbados.[20]

Many vessels from ports to the westward that were bound for Boston called at Newport to discharge or take on cargo; and more

19. Newbury-Richardson Commonplace Book, 1687–17__ (MS, NHS), n.p., 1684–89, *passim; RIHS Colls.,* XXIV, 89, 91.

20. *Sanford Letter Book,* iii–vi, 14–15.

than a few Massachusetts coasters entered on voyages to Connecticut and New Haven for wheat and flour, or to Long Island for whale oil. At the same time Rhode Islanders, among them Providence Williams, son of Roger, were plying back and forth to Boston or up and down Long Island Sound carrying miscellaneous freights and commissions. A glimpse of the kinds of cargoes that William and Christopher Almy and fellow coasters freighted can be gained from a manifest of the brigantine *Prosperous*, John Prentice, commander, laden at Boston by Thomas Palmer, merchant, and bound "for Rode Island in New England, Bristoll, New London, or Long Island etc., upon a trading voyage": two chests, one box, one trunk, and "2 casque of Nayles with four Chest of English Goods, and four pipes of wine, in all Nineteen parcels," as entered at His Majesty's Customs for the account of John Carson. (Before the eighties, it should be pointed out, no coaster would have had to clear out.) [21]

After the end of King Philip's War, so many open boats, decked sloops, barques, and larger ships plied the waters of Rhode Island Sound that the fourth book of *The English Pilot* (1689) included "Directions for Sailing into several Ports in New-England. By Capt. John Prents [Prence of Plymouth?]." It contained, for the first time, a description of Narragansett Bay for mariners but, strangely, omitted the course into Newport: "This Bay lying in the North, betwixt the Point of Conanecut and Point Judeth, avoiding one Rock called the Whale, sail on either side of the Rock, and anchor at pleasure; If you would sail in at the East-end of Road-Island, you will see divers high Rocks upon the Starboard-

21. John Garde, a Newport shipowner and merchant sold his ship *Exchange*, 90 tons, with all of its gear for £700 current money of New England to William Titherly, who had recently moved from "Bye the Ford," county Devon, to Boston. *Suffolk Deeds*, VII, 71; Richard Smith, Jr., to Fitz-John Winthrop, April 15, 1675, Winthrop MSS (MHS), XVIII, 102; John Hull, Letter Book, 1670–1685 (MS, typed copy in American Antiquarian Society, Worcester), 269–70; Stevens, Transcripts, III, no. 177; Connecticut Archives, Trade (MS, State Library, Hartford), 1st ser., I, 33b.

side a mile from Shore, sail within a Mile of those Rocks N. and N. Westerly a League in, in the middle of the Channel is good anchoring for all Winds but a Southerly Wind; it is Navigable round about Road-Island, keeping in the middle of the Channel."[22]

Under the careful management of the Quaker merchants, most of the shipping dispatched after 1660 went down Long Island Sound to Manhattan Island, the Jerseys, the valley of the Delaware, and seaports farther south. Often, too, the merchants combined the voyages with others to the Wine Islands or Europe. The Richardsons' account book is full of data about these expeditions; one can virtually follow the Quaker take-over of trade with Manhattan in the very years (1662–69) that New Netherland was being transformed into New York. There the Quakers dealt extensively with Dutch merchants who, lacking ships, sorely needed English connections. Nicholas Davis of Hyannis and Newport figured prominently in reorienting this trade and bringing the brothers into contact with Frederick Phillipse, Gerrit van Tright, Jeronimus Ebbling, John Potts, and the Huguenots Peter and Nicholas Bayard and Gabriel Minvielle. Vessels from Rhode Island unladed some of their cargo at Manhattan and took aboard European goods, wines, and other items supplied by the Dutch merchants, who knew from long experience what would sell best to the Chesapeake planters. The Richardsons sent *Tryall* to Manhattan and Virginia with goods consigned to them by Rhode Islanders, who paid them for carrying their rundlets, barrels, and hogsheads. Thus the merchants profited both by the sale of their goods and by the

22. Captain Prents warned against Buzzard's Bay, "which is a very foul Bay." He also advised mariners sailing to Long Island from the eastward "to come not northward of Latitude 40° [actually 41°] because of danger on "Nantucket Sholes." *The English Pilot, The Fourth Book* (London, 1689), facsimile ed. by Coolie Verner, Theatrum Orbis Terrarum, 4th ser., I (Amsterdam, 1969), 49–50. See also the Draught of the Narragansett River (July 1684), in Stevens, Transcripts, II, 177a, which shows the coast from Stonington to Cape Cod, including the towns of Newport, Portsmouth, Swansea, Rehoboth, King's Town, Narragansett, and Providence.

freight charges. Such a satisfactory arrangement was possible because the New Yorkers no longer commanded the shipping of the West India Company after 1664.[23]

Toward the end of the seventies, the trade in wines and liquors attracted merchants doing business with Manhattan. Walter Newbury of Rhode Island imported them for New Yorkers through the agency of his recent London associates. He shipped on *Sarah* in December 1676 eight pipes of Fayal and two pipes of green Canary wine; and one month later, by Christopher Almy, he sent fourteen hogsheads and four quarter casks of brandy to Frederick Phillipse and William Richardson, who was now living in New York. Less than two weeks later, to Phillipse by Almy went another shipment of Canary in four butts and four Spanish wine pipes, along with one butt of wine for Robert LaRoque. There is very little evidence of consignments of wines and brandies from Boston to Newport, whose traders procured them sometimes at Newfoundland, but probably more often in the West Indies. It is not without significance that John Champlin, "late of Fayall," joined the merchants of Rhode Island in 1675; unfortunately his papers have not survived. There is no shadow of doubt whatever that the Rhode Island merchants had fine wines and liquors for sale in quantity, as well as strong beer and fiery rum.[24]

Everywhere along the coastal trade routes from Piscataqua as far south as Delaware Bay, wool from Rhode Island was eagerly sought, as were barreled mutton and, in several communities, Narragansett sheep for breeding. To John Robinson of New York Walter New-

23. This paragraph and succeeding ones are based principally upon William and Thomas Richardson, Account Book, 1662–69, and Thomas Richardson, Account Book (MSS, NHS), both unpaged.

24. Another possible clue to the wine trade of Rhode Island is that in these years a John Gard[e], an English merchant, was residing at Horta in the Azores; he may have been a relative of the ship captain of the same name at Newport. See Duncan T. Bentley, *Atlantic Islands: Madeira, the Azores, and the Cape Verdes in Seventeenth-Century Commerce and Navigation* (Chicago, 1972), 150–56; *RIHS Colls.*, XXIV, 82, 84.

bury shipped five bags of wool weighing a total of 760 pounds, and, a few months later, another 100 pounds. When numbers of Friends settled in West New Jersey and Pennsylvania, Thomas Budd of Burlington provided them with some useful information and advice in *Good Order Established* (1685): "But it may be queried, Where shall Wool be gotten to carry the Woollen Manufacture, until we have of our own raising? I answer; in Road-Island, and some other adjacent Islands and Places, Wool may be bought at six Pence a Pound, and considerable Quantities may be there had, which will supply until we can raise enough of our own." The good Quaker took his own advice a year later by purchasing some wool and six hogsheads of rum from Walter Newbury. A few years before this, Newbury had shipped "twenty Six horse kind and fifty five sheep with the Provision Customary" in the ketch *Merchant Adventure* to Joseph Morton in Carolina. It was at this time (1682) that Samuel Wilson was reporting that "Ewes have most commonly two or three Lambs at a time; their Wool is good Staple and they thrive well...."[25]

Trade followed the meeting wherever the Friends went in the New World. Thomas Richardson prepared an accounting on November 13, 1668, of "our first winter in Maryland," which listed the names and places of residence of thirty-eight Quaker planters and the amounts (in pounds of tobacco) they owed for goods purchased from the partners. One account was for John Richardson, planter, who may have been a kinsman. When the farmers of Rhode Island gave up the growing of tobacco after the mid-century, William Brenton immediately sensed the opportunity of trading his own produce for either Sweet-Scented or Oronoco

25. Alexander S. Salley, ed., *Narratives of Early Carolina, 1650–1708,* Original Narratives of Early American History, ed. J. Franklin Jameson (New York, 1911), 172; *RIHS Colls.,* XXIV, 83, 84, 87, 89; Thomas Budd, *Good Order Established in Pensilvania and New Jersey in America* (London, 1685), 11–12.

leaf sold by the merchant-planter Colonel Edmund Scarborough, a wealthy Anglican living on the Eastern Shore of Virginia. Beginning in 1663, so many Quakers settled along there—and as far northward as the head of the Chesapeake—and were raising tobacco that Friends of Rhode Island took advantage of the Navigation Laws and moved in to pick up lucrative cargoes that formerly had gone in Dutch vessels to New Amsterdam. William Garde of Newport continued to deal with the Anglican Scarborough as late as 1668.[26]

Apparently the Richardsons reduced their trade with the Virginia planters and moved up Chesapeake Bay to concentrate on the Maryland Friends. In 1669 there were only thirty-five Bay planters in their debt, but they, however, owed a total of 24,400 pounds of tobacco. Among the planters who traded with the Rhode Islanders were George Skipwith of West River, Thomas Skillington, "John Moors [Morse?] of the Clifts," William Collier of Rhoad River, and John Collier of Bush River, where they also dealt with Jan Jansen, "Dutchman" (or Swede). From their small-draft ketches and sloops, which could go up shallow rivers and creeks, the Narragansett traders sold them, and other Chesapeake tobacco growers, barreled salt pork and beef, horses, candles, strong beer, barrels of tar, wooden "stooles," new empty barrels and other casks (some with iron hoops), and all from Rhode Island; from Manhattan they procured and sold "bisket," flour, hardware and nails, lead, woolens and linens, canvas, wines and brandy. They

26. The Navigation Act of 1660 made tobacco an enumerated article that had to be carried from any colony in English- or plantation-built vessels manned by predominantly English crews. The effect was to give New England shipping an unexpected advantage. See William Macdonald, ed., *Select Charters and Other Documents Illustrative of American History, 1606–1775* (New York, 1899), 110, 119, 133. *Suffolk Deeds*, I, 290–91; *Records of the Court of Trials*, 70, 76, 80; Richardson, Account Book, 1662–1702, Nov. 16, 1668.

also disposed of large quantities of Tortuga salt by the bushel, Muscovado sugar, and rum brought from the English or Dutch islands of the Caribbean to Newport. Moving in the tributaries, big and little, of the Chesapeake Bay, these tiny craft were an early maritime equivalent of the general store.[27]

All transactions in the Chesapeake area were handled by exchange of goods; no money or bills of exchange seem to have passed hands. When William Richardson sold a mare to William Nicholas from Bristol in November 1669, he took his pay in European goods. The Marylanders settled all of their accounts with merchantable tobacco in cask or in "dry hydes." When the Richardson brothers sailed back to New York with a hold filled with these two commodities, they sold them to pay for the goods they had picked up there to take to Maryland. Any surplus that remained they used to buy such English goods as they would otherwise have had to get at Boston, probably at higher prices. The ketch now and then carried passengers to and fro; in October 1668 they brought a Negro named Sambo in addition to the twenty-five hogsheads of Sweet-Scented leaf consigned to the Bayards.[28]

COMMERCE between Rhode Island and Barbados antedated the arrival of the Friends at Newport. John Throgmorton and Randall Holden were partners in the cargo of the barque *Deborah*, most of which was sold at Bridgetown about 1656; the remainder was

27. Thomas Richardson, Account Book, 1669.

28. The papers of William Brenton of Boston, Newport, and Taunton would have told us more about the economy of all New England, 1638 to 1674, than almost any others, had they survived. This ubiquitous trader made William Sanford his attorney to sue in the Charles County Court in 1663 for all debts due him in Virginia, as well as in Maryland. Sanford also sued on his own for payment by William Battin for nails, axes, iron pots, and horn combs. There is little doubt that the ironware came from Taunton, where Brenton had access to the products of Raynham Furnace. *Archives of Maryland*, LIII, 339–40, 366, 397, 398.

left there with Mark Hands, a Boston trader who had long resided in the island. On December 17, 1661, William Brenton, who had been dealing with the Barbadians for several years, gave a power of attorney to his twenty-two-year-old ward and future son-in-law Peleg Sanford to collect all debts due from the Barbadians and sent him to Bridgetown to learn all he could about the trading opportunities opened up by the "sugar revolution." Peleg became associated with Mark Hands, and, when the latter returned to Boston, Peleg took over several of Hands's accounts. After a stay of five years, the young man sailed home to Newport and set up as a merchant. Most of his dealings were with a younger brother, William, who had established himself at Bridgetown. By keeping the traffic between the West Indies and Rhode Island open, these two brothers made a vital link in the Hutchinson family's chain of mercantile enterprises reaching from Boston to London.[29]

In the mid-fifties, Barbados was the center for Quakers in the New World. Within a few years, differences in attitudes on varying social matters stirred up animosities among the people, and the government and the Church found the Quakers very troublesome. Many Friends, suffering from persecution, migrated to Rhode Island, where both the physical and religious climate were more congenial. Nevertheless, the enterprising Richardsons and Friend Nicholas Davis shared in a voyage of the ketch *Tryall* to Barbados in 1662–63, and other Quakers, among them Richard Borden, were shortly importing small quantities of Barbadian goods, probably cotton and sugar. After a few years, Borden's son Joseph went to

29. The Town Meeting at Portsmouth voted on January 23, 1654/5 "to pay ould John motts passage to the Barbadoes Iland and back againe if he Cannot be received there, if he live to it, if the Shippe owner will carrie him." *Portsmouth Recs.*, 66; R.I. Land Evidences (photostats, vault M, W31, RIHS), 65–68; *CSM Pubs.*, XXIX, 50; *President John Sanford of . . . Portsmouth, Rhode Island* (Rutland, Vt., 1966), xiv, xv, 7; *New England Historical and Genealogical Register*, LXVIII, 179; *Sanford Letter Book*, iv, vi.

the Caribbean to settle permanently. He and his second wife, Ann, made their residence at Bridgetown the acknowledged clearing-house (and boardinghouse) for Quaker merchants and mariners from New England.[30]

About the year 1667 an incident occurred that in itself was un-important, but it does reveal the continuing antipathy of some of the Puritans in the Bay Colony toward the Quakers. William Coddington and other Friends attempted in that year to import from London by way of Barbados some Quaker books that had cost £10 sterling in England. By mistake they were sent to Piscataqua, where they were seized by some Massachusetts magistrates and taken by them to Boston. After an exchange of arguments extend-ing over five years and the refusal of his old friend Governor Richard Bellingham to give them to Coddington, the latter taunted him in *A Demonstration of True Love,* published at London in 1672. First stating that even the Spanish papists at Málaga would merely have detained such books until a ship was ready to send them on, Coddington demanded that the man whom he had entertained and for whose spiritual comfort he had arranged to have a Congregational service at his house in Newport submit the issue to arbitration "as in [the] Lex Mercatoria, the Law amongst Merchants." Incredible as it appears, he got no satisfaction.[31]

Ketches and sloops from Providence, as well as Newport, now became familiar sights in Carlisle Bay and, though less frequently, in the roadsteads of Antigua, Nevis, and Saint Christopher. Several mercantile Friends at Bridgetown had discovered the worth of

30. *New England Historical and Genealogical Register,* LXVIII, 181; Rich-ardson, Account Book, 1662–63, *passim.* On the Friends in the West Indies and their early trade to New England, see Carl and Roberta Bridenbaugh, *No Peace Beyond the Line: The English in the Caribbean, 1624–1690* (New York, 1972), 357–59, 386–93, 397–98.

31. William Coddington, *A Demonstration of True Love* (London, 1674), 7, 11–12.

Narragansett-built ships, among them William Boseman, who instructed Captain Samuel Venner to go to Rhode Island in 1671 with a bill of exchange "payable to one Sarah Reape," from whom he hoped to buy a ship. This might have been the ketch her husband commanded four years before. Most of the ships, though not all, were sent down by Quaker merchants under Quaker masters with consignments to Friends in the islands. An unidentified Connecticut correspondent informed Governor John Winthrop, Jr., from Barbados in February 1675 that the Quakers there were "a people . . . very welthy and numerous, being above one third of the island of that tenent, and dayly getting new converts." [32]

Walter Newbury, who has figured prominently in these exchanges, was an active young Friend and "London merchant" of twenty-four when he crossed the Atlantic to Rhode Island in 1673. One year later he bought from William Richardson (by now trading at New York) a large waterfront property at Newport consisting of land, timber, woods, a mansion with a garden, "Ware-Houses, Wharfeige, Cellars, etc.," where he conducted his business and served the Society of Friends in many ways. Immediately upon his arrival at Newport, he began to trade with Barbadian Quaker merchants, one of whom, Oliver Hooton, became an intimate friend of the family. Walter Newbury's shipping book is the prime source for the study of West Indian trade, which reached its peak at this time. [33]

32. *Suffolk Deeds*, VII, 283–84; *Calendar of State Papers, Colonial, 1661–1668*, p. 71; *MHS Procs.*, 2d ser., VII, 16–17; Providence Town Papers (MS, RIHS), I, 57; Daniel B. Updike, *Richard Smith* . . . (Boston, 1937), 87–92.

33. "The Walter Newbury Shipping Book" covers the years 1672 to 1689 and is printed in *RIHS Colls.*, XXIV, 73–91. It consists of the usual London-printed forms of the day bound together. The transcriber did not copy the package marks and parcel identifications written on the left-hand margin of each page, or the freight rates (generally in pounds of sugar) or the stipulated condition of the outsides and insides of the casks. There are several errors in the transcription, and the student of commerce will want

Before 1690, certainly, the oft-rehearsed schoolbook story about the "triangular trade" from New England (including Rhode Island) to the West Indies, to London, then home again is pure myth. It was almost totally a down-and-back traffic. The most significant feature about it economically was the extraordinary diversity of the cargoes shipped from Newport to the Caribbean, and generally speaking, the restriction of returns to four West Indian staples: rum, cotton wool, molasses, and Muscovado sugar—in that order of importance usually. Many vessels returned in ballast or else sailed all the way to the Spanish Main to take on much-neeeded salt at Tortuga. When Governor Peleg Sanford reported to the Lords of Trade and Plantations in 1680 that "the principall matters that are exported amongst us, is Horses and provisions, and the goods chiefly imported is a small quantity of Barbados goods for the supply of our familyes," he gave no indication of the volume and nature of the produce of his colony. The shipping records of Peleg Sanford himself, 1662–68, before he became governor, and far more those of Walter Newbury, 1672–89, taken with other scattered evidence, reveal that the livestock, agricultural, forest, and local marine produce from the colony and adjacent areas totaled thirty-six items, all of them staples in the West Indian trade.[34]

When advices about prices were lacking—Caribbean markets were occasionally glutted—a ship's master with a mixed cargo, miscellaneous though it might be, often stood a better chance of making a paying voyage than one carrying a single item. Some shipments chosen at random illustrate what kind of cargoes Rhode Island vessels carried. Late in 1673 Joseph Borden and Richard Sander of Bridgetown received from Walter Newbury seven firkins of butter, seven bars of iron, and forty-four boxes of pills. At another time the Newporter dispatched to Joseph Grove and Oliver

to see the original at NHS. See *ibid.*, 75–78, 81; *R.I. Land Evidences*, I, 94; *Timehri*, n.s., X (1896), 117; Records of the Quarterly Meeting of Rhode Island from 1681 to 1746 inclusive: Minutes (MSS, RIHS), 4, 6.

34. Stevens, Transcripts, I, no. 154.

Hooton two barrels of beef, and one of mutton; and to Timothy Marshall, one barrel of beef, one barrel of mutton, and a barrel of "Hodgs fatt." In 1682 Newbury sent by Joseph Bryer, master of *Portsmouth*, the following miscellany to Dr. Thomas Rodman (who had not yet forsaken Bridgetown for Newport):

4 barrels of pork	3 barrels of cider
6 firkins of soap	2 chests of candles
10 barrels of tar	

The largest variety of goods went to Jamaica in 1678 and 1684. The first shipment went at Newbury's own risk, but the second (the list follows) was shared by his kinsman Benjamin Newbury:

50	barrels of mackerel	5	whole, and
51	whole, and	30	half barrels of flour
40	half barrels of pork	100	barrels of tar
8	barrels, and	61	firkins of butter
40	half barrels of beef	2	barrels of [train] oil
20	barrels of cider	14	hogsheads of fish
9	barrels of beer	9	firkins of hog's fat [lard]
2	hogsheads, and	10	boxes of candles
9	barrels of onions	1,540	staves
12	hogsheads of biscuit	8	casks of apples
		50	cheeses[35]

With the establishment of the Dominion of New England, Rhode Island vessels were expected to enter and clear at Boston, and the records of the British Customs consequently supply us with further information on Rhode Island ventures to the West Indies. Daniel Gould, whose name appears frequently, was not only active in the Newport Monthly Meeting, but he was also one of the leading ship captains of New England. He owned the sloop *Betty*

35. *RIHS Colls.*, XXIV, 80, 85, 86, 87, 89. Peleg Sanford's shipments were much less miscellaneous but of the same general composition. *Sanford Letter Book*, 7–72, and "Index of Subjects," pp. 82–84.

of Rhode Island in 1685 when he entered Nevis with the following cargo:

6 barrels of beef	20 barrels of cider
45 barrels of pork	3 chests of candles
18 firkins of butter	6 cheeses

2,000 staves

When he entered at Nevis in 1687, he had a new and larger vessel that was carrying 18 horses, 15,000 staves, and 6,000 shingles. The cargo he took to Boston from the Leeward Islands the following year he obviously planned to sell there because it contained so much sugar, an article that seldom sold well in his home port:

2 hogsheads of sugar	26 bags of cotton wool
4 casks of sugar	8 packs of cotton wool
21 kilderkins of sugar	62 hogsheads of rum
7 barrels of tobacco	60 barrels of rum
25 barrels of molasses	66 hogsheads of molasses[36]

Up to this point, little mention has been made of shipments of livestock from Rhode Island to the Caribbean. The herds and flocks fed the West Indians in the form of butter, cheese, lard, and salted pork, beef, and mutton, but animals with heavy coats and acclimated to the mild weather of the Narragansett Bay region could not be expected to survive for very long, let alone flourish, in the tropics. Peleg Sanford did send down some cattle on at least one voyage, and Walter Newbury risked a few with Oliver Hooton in 1684 and twenty-three more with Joseph Grove in Barbados in 1687. The story was entirely different with horses, for they were needed continually to turn the sugar mills and provide the planters with saddle mounts.[37]

Shortly after Peleg Sanford began his sojourn at Bridgetown,

36. Public Record Office, London: C. O. 5/848, p. 5; 157/1, pp. 99a, 160a.

37. *Sanford Letter Book*, 23; *RIHS Colls.*, XXIV, 87, 90. For horses, see Bridenbaugh, *No Peace Beyond the Line*, index, s.v. "Horses."

he must have run into Captain Alexander of the great ship *Black Horse*, out of Topsham but last from Amsterdam, with a crew of thirty-two men and a cargo of fifty-two horses bred in North Holland. When he arrived in Carlisle Bay late in December 1661, there was no cotton or sugar available for a return cargo to Europe. The resourceful master of *Black Horse* accepted the advice of his factor—and possibly young Sanford—and cleared out January 11, 1661/2 for "Read Iland" or "Rohte Insul," where horses were both plentiful and cheap. Making port in Narragansett Bay, he unladed his cargo of salt and the sand used for ballast, and took on staves, salted meat, meal, and bread. Then, along with fresh water and hay (which was bound together in bales so that it could be handled), thirty fine horses were brought on board on March 4. *Black Horse* sailed on March 6 but lost a mast 450 miles from its destination and had to return to Newport because of contrary winds. A mast was soon secured and refitted, and after additional fresh water and hay for the horses was taken aboard, the 400-ton ship set off once more and arrived in Bridgetown on April 30 in good condition, with the loss of only one horse.[38]

Occasional shipments of horses had taken place in small colonial vessels before *Black Horse* called at Newport; after 1662 they became a profitable staple. Seldom anticipated by other merchants, the Richardsons and Nicholas Davis sent *Tryall* on two voyages in 1663–64 with sixteen horses each time—a full cargo for their ketch, considering the casks of water and bales of hay required. The freight, passage, and food amounted to £12 a horse, plus 9d. for carrying it ashore. As one might expect, Peleg Sanford shipped many Rhode Island–bred horses, mares, and geldings procured from the farms of the Hutchinsons and John Hull to Barbados between 1662 and 1668. Usually Henry Beare carried them in his

38. Although Captain Alexander lost half of his Dutch horses on the Atlantic crossing, he sold the remainder at a profit. Felix Christian Spörri, *Americanische Reiss-beschreibung Nach den Caribes Insslen, Und Neu-Engelland* (Zurich, 1677), 29, 32, 43, 47; also *NEQ*, X, 544–45.

ketch, and at Bridgetown William Sanford sold them, ordinarily for 2,000 pounds of sugar a head.[39]

The 1670's brought a great demand in the West Indies for all sorts of animals, which spurred Walter Newbury on to sending horses, together with oats, hay, corn, and water casks, "as Customary," to his Quaker agents in Barbados to sell to the sugar planters. Edward Thorn, a far-from-trustworthy overseer for Christopher Jeaffreson, the absentee owner of a large estate on Saint Christopher, sailed to Rhode Island in December 1679, where he purchased thirteen horses and mares. This turned out to be a fortunate venture, for he lost only one animal on the voyage back and sold the rest "at high prices." From the rising village of Bristol on Narragansett Bay in 1686, the first consignment of horses sailed in the *Bristol Merchant* to the Dutch colony of Surinam. Most merchants were loath to risk in their cargoes more than one horse to £30 worth of provisions. Diversity remained their watchword.[40]

A letter young William Wilkinson in Barbados wrote home to his Quaker parents in Providence in 1708—it could just as well have been written before 1690—epitomizes in very human terms how the Friends, their ships, the sea, and the equine denizens of the colony combined to bring it substantial prosperity:

39. One must keep in mind in this connection that the merchants of Boston and New London shipped out hundreds of horses raised in Rhode Island. Richardson, Account Book, 1662–69, July 5, 1663, and the accounts of the ketch *Tryall* for 1664; *Sanford Letter Book*, 7, 8, 21–23, 26, 29–33, 43, 69–72.

40. Samuel Wilson wrote from Charles Town in 1682: "There have been imported into Carolina about an hundred and fifty Mares and some Horses from New-York and Rhoad Island, which breed well and the Coalts they have are finer Lim'd and Headed than their Dams or Sires. . . ." Salley, ed., *Narratives of Early Carolina*, 172, 184; *RIHS Colls.*, XXIV, 80, 87, 88, 89, 90, 91; John C. Jeaffreson, ed., *A Young Squire of the Seventeenth Century, from the Papers of Christopher Jeaffreson* . . . (London, 1878), I, 253–54; Federal Writers' Project, *Rhode Island: A Guide to the Smallest State* (Boston, 1937), 184; *Providence Recs.*, XV, 91–92.

"Honored Father and Mother,

"I think it my duty to write to you at this time and let you know that I am indifferently well in health at this time. Blessed be God for it, and [I] am safe arrived at Barbados, although we had a long and tedious passage of 33 days, and a long storm, for we sailed the 10th day of the first Month and the wind at west and be south, and on the 11th at night the wind blew a storm so that we could not bear no knot of sail, but drive before it; and we was drove on the banks called Saint Georges Banks lying 30 or 40 miles to the east-ward of Nantucket, where the waves run like fire in the night. And they flung overboard some of the hens, and would have flung over the horses had they their will; but Ephraim [an older Quaker supercargo] would not consent till it was day, and then we got over the banks and had sea room enough. And so we run eastward 11 or 12 days, and could scarce make any sail nor keep any reckon-ing how far we run, but we conclude we run 20 degrees eastward before we got 4 [degrees] south, and an exceeding great sea run that broke over the stern and broke the breastwork of the vessel, and killed one horse and made the rest poor. They talked very often [of] flinging them overboard, but still we persuaded them to keep them a little longer; and so we kept them all but one. The 13th of the 2d Month we got on shore on Barbados, and I perceiving there was two vessels going for New England, one to Boston and the other to Rhoad Island, I think to send by them both that so you may hear. As for news out of this country, all things that are brought out of New England are very low except hogs, which are more than ordinary high at this time. The commodities of this country are also low. The weather is very hot and dry, so that it makes one faint. The small pox is also here, not 3 or 4 [people] break out yet, for it's but newly come."

"This I say not to scare you, for as for me, I am freely given into the hand of God for him to do with me as pleaseth him, whether in sickness or health, life or death; and I don't report my coming, but as to my coming home at this time, I cannot say much, but expect to write again when I know more, hoping that I shall see you again, if it be the will of God. But if otherwise, I desire you to be comforted, for it is most certain that we must part one time or other, and my desire is that whenever it be that it may be for the better. So remember me to my Brothers and Sisters, all my relations and friends, telling them that I have not forgot them, hoping that they are in health. I think to write to Joseph Smith. I lodge at Ann Borden's in the Bridgetown, she being the second wife of Joseph Borden, where I want for nothing the Island affords. So no more at present, my love to you,

"WILLIAM WILKINSON

"Tell Thomas Hopkins I am not enough acquainted with people here to direct him [how] to consign hogs, but they are £35 a thousand [weight], which [is] a very great price, but there is a fleet expected from England and it may be after they won't be half so high

"To Samuel Wilkinson, Providence
By Captain Rugels"[41]

41. William Wilkinson, Bridgetown, Barbados, to Samuel Wilkinson, Providence, April 20, 1708 (MS in possession of Bradford Swan, Providence).

CONCLUSION

IN the year 1690, the colony of Rhode Island and Providence Plantations presented a far different picture from that sketched by both its enemies and by many historians since then. Agriculturally and commercially it was a highly successful undertaking—one almost says spectacularly so—and far from the misgoverned, immoral, disjointed society of ignorant clowns harboring blasphemous religious opinions that its fearful and jealous neighbors branded it. More than half of the inhabitants had joined the Society of Friends, whose members notoriously had one foot in the meetinghouse and the other in the countinghouse. Concentrated on the islands and the Narragansett shore, rich Antinomian exiles from the Bay Colony had by this time become Quaker farmers, sea captains, and merchants who, collectively, had performed the remarkable feat of transforming themselves from English grain growers into colonial graziers and marketers. The breeding and raising of hogs, cattle, sheep, and horses enabled the Rhode Islanders to pay for their modest importations of much-needed European goods and, in a few instances, some desired luxuries. They also managed to garner a small but steady profit, which they used to extend their agricultural activities, invest in more land, purchase shares in colony-built ships, and, not infrequently, save in the form of ready cash, silver, and gold. The entire undertaking had created wealth where, before 1636, none at all had existed. This was no small accomplishment.

While the authorities at Whitehall were devising a new government for Massachusetts Bay, New Hampshire, and Maine in 1686, Joseph Dudley wrote to Secretary Blathwayt urging the inclusion of Rhode Island and Connecticut in the proposed Dominion of New England. For, said he, these "are the Principall parts of the Countrey where Corne and Cattle [by which he meant all four-footed beasts] are raised for the supply of the Great Trade of fishing and Other Shipping belonging to this his Majesty's Territory." Evidently the Bay merchants still coveted Naboth's Meadows in Rhode Island and Providence Plantations. Dudley knew full well that without the agricultural surpluses of these two colonies the Bostonians could not continue to maintain their "Trade with bread."[1]

Boston was what the economists call a parasite port, and among the principal hosts upon which it fastened, sucked, and climbed were the wheat and corn of Connecticut and the corn and livestock of Rhode Island. The important role of the former is well known; Rhode Island's, for some reason, has never been chronicled. In return for the provisions they drew in from farmers of southern New England, the Bostonians sold them some clothing of English make, hardware, and other necessary goods (never in very large quantities), always at a very substantial profit.

Lest this appear to be an ex parte case, made out perhaps from an excess of local pride, it may be concluded with the testimony of two highly competent observers of that time, neither of them warmed by the holy heat of Puritanism nor bitter about the kinds of imperialism practiced or attempted in the cause of Godliness by the men of Massachusetts Bay. An anonymous writer declared in 1690 that "Road-Island is of a considerable bigness, and justly called THE GARDEN OF NEW ENGLAND, for its Fertility and Pleasant-

1. Gay Collection of Transcripts relating to the History of New England, 1660–1776 (MHS) State Papers, VI, 89; R. N. Toppan and A. T. S. Goodrick, *Edward Randolph* . . . , Prince Society Publications (Boston, 1898–1909), VI, 196.

ness. It abounds with all Things necessary for the life of Man, is excellent for Sheep, Kine, and Horses; and being environed by the Sea, it is freed from the dangers of Bears, Wolves, and Foxes, which much molest and damnifie those that live on the Continent. . . . The People live in great plenty, send Horses and Provisions to Barbados, and the Leeward-Islands, and sell great numbers of fat oxen and Sheep to the Butchers of Boston."[2]

Dr. Benjamin Bullivant, an observant, cultivated gentleman, familiar with English, as well as with colonial, husbandry, visited "the Isle of Error" in June 1697. Upon reaching Newport by road, he wrote, "you enter by a Curious playne or Common, on which you see feedding good store of Neate cattle, and sheepe. . . . Here [in Newport] are some Merchants, and shopkeepers, whc live plentifully and easily, the Island affording most excellent provisions of all kind, the people Courteous and obligeing to strangers, the farmes for Largenesse, and goodness of pasturadge, excelling any-thing I ever saw in New England, and they produce in each farme wood enough to shelter theyr cattle in the Sumer heates, and warme theyr chimnies in the winter cold. Theyr dairies may equall if not exceed, the best yeomen's farmes in England. Some have made 90 £ per annum from theyr dairie alone, and on one farme have shorne upwards of 1000 sheepe, and sold every pound of wool for 10s per to ready money [hard silver], it being much wanted by all people, as excelling any that is showne on the Continent. . . . We bought choyce Veale by the quarter for 2d the pound, theyr mutton was pure good—theyr butter and cheese excellent and their wine [imported from Fayal or the Canaries], beere and cyder, very commendable—Exceeding much fish."[3]

Thus it fell out that by 1690 the Antinomian-Quaker first gentle-men of Rhode Island—Coddington, Brenton, Harding, Coggeshall

2. *A Short Account of the Present State of New England* (London, 1690), 1–3.

3. Writing in 1687, a Huguenot settled in the Narragansett Country said of Aquidneck: "This Island, they tell me, is well-settled, and with a great

and others, the Congregational Sanfords, and even the Anglican Francis Brinley—had become the first American stockmen and the founders on the western shore of the bay of what, in the eighteenth century, was the group called the Narragansett Planters. It was these men and their less affluent fellow farmers of several faiths who made the grazing industry the prime source of wealth —the capital—that built the commercial republic of Rhode Island in the next century.

In these pages history has been turned around. It was not, as has always been taught, that the failure of farming drove the men of the Narragansett region down to the sea; rather it was the prospect of marketing a lucrative agricultural surplus at Boston, New York, and in the southern colonies and the West Indies that forced local merchants to build wharves and warehouses, to acquire or construct ketches, barques, and sloops for the youth of the colony to sail to faraway ports. HOPE (their motto of 1647) was translated into reality in seventeenth-century Rhode Island and Providence Plantations; and that reality rested solidly upon fat mutton and liberty of conscience.

Trade, which I know of my own Knowledge." *Report of a Protestant Refugee, in Boston, 1687*, E. T. Fisher, trans. (Brooklyn, 1868), 19. Unfortunately the Huguenot's letter about Rhode Island was lost. "Travel Diary of Dr. Benjamin Bullivant [1697]," in *New-York Historical Society Quarterly*, XL, 58–60.

APPENDICES

APPENDIX I

LANDHOLDING AT

NEWPORT AND PORTSMOUTH

1639–1640

THE following list indicates the wide range of grants and also the great care taken in recording at Aquidneck. It is compiled from Horace E. Turner, Abstract of Colonial Land Evidences (Rhode Island), Book I (MS in NHS); the page numbers are those of the original records.

Name	Number of acres	Page
1. William Coddington	730	26
2. William Brenton	399	21
3. Nicholas Easton	389	23
4. John Coggeshall	389 (actually 369)	21
5. Thomas Burton	304	46
6. Robert Harding	300	47
7. John Porter	235	49
8. William Foster	228½	24, 45, 60
9. Thomas Brassie	200	48
10. Jeremy Clarke	186½	23
11. Dr. John Clarke	158	65
Dr. John Clarke	148	22
12. William Dyer	110	43
William Dyer	87	22
13. Richard Hayward [?]	88	49
14. George Gardner (Portsmouth)	76	51
George Gardner	58	24

Name	Number of acres	Page
15. Robert Field	75	25
Robert Field	65	45
16. John Hall	67	48
17. Robert Stanton	58	24
18. Joseph Clarke	50	65
19. Thomas Clarke	48	55
20. Thomas Spicer	45	50
21. John Vaughan (laborer)	42	66
22. Jeoffrey Champlin and		
23. Richard Serle	40	56
24. John Peckham	40	52
25. Mary Clarke	40	52
26. Robert Carr	40	53
27. Marmaduke Ward	40	53
28. Richard Maxson	36	54
29. Lambert and Henry Woodward	20	24
30. William Cowley	20	54
31. Thomas Stafford	17	55
32. Edward Andrews	13½	51
33. Thomas Beeder	13	61
34. Edward Browne	10½	60
35. Robert Bennett ("Taylor")	10	62
36. John Thornton (servant)	10	62
37. John Frees ("Thatcher")	10	46
38. Job Hawkins	9	61
39. Edward Browce	4 (house lot)	60

APPENDIX II

GEORGE FOX'S

LETTER TO

RHODE ISLAND

OFFICIALS

1672

THE Law of God that answereth that of God in every one, and bringeth every one to doe that to others, as they would have others doe to them.

A Law against Drunkeness, and them that Sell liquors to make People Drunk.

A Law against fighting and Swearing.

And all your ancient Liberties looked into and Priviledges and agreements concerning your Divine Liberty and National Liberty, and all your outward liberties and priviledges of your Comons that belong to your Towne, Island, and Colony be looked into.

And that you have a Markett once a weeke in your Towne [Newport], and a house built for that purpose, least your Enemies boast over you that would have done itt as is pretended.

And that in Every Towne and place in all your Colony one to Receive all your Births, Marriages, and them that dye, and Record them which might doe well and Lett not your ancient Liberties [and] Priviledges bee trodden downe, but minde that which is for the good of your Colonie, and the Comonwealth of all People, and that is not for their hurt nor your owne; And be sure to fasten Soe that you may answer that of God in all People, then you answer God in your places; And when you Judge of matters or when you judge of words or when you Judge of Persons all those are distinct things, doe not give both your Ears, lett him have one, and Reserve the other for the other, and then judge of the matter against Sin and Oppression, and Stand up for the good of the people which is for the good of your Selves.

Lett all the people Know their Rights and Priviledges for now may you make or marr, and therefore now stand up for the glory of God that it may Shine over your Colony, and now if you doe not that which is right and wise and outstrip them that have gone before you, them that you are over the old Government will laugh att you, which I would not have to bee; And all the wisest are loving or convinced in your Colony, and therfore stand together for Gods glory and your owne, and the peoples good, and take of[f] all oppressions in your Colony and Sett up Justice over all your Colony and that will bee a praise to them that doe well; and a Terror to the Evill doers, and what an Honor is itt that Christ should bee both Priest, Prophett, Minister, Shepherd, and Bishop, Councellor, Leader, and Captaine and Prince in your Colony, and you may Praise God for Ever and stand fast in the Liberty wherewith Christ hath made you free in Life, Glory, and Power.

You are the unworthiest Men upon the Earth if you doe loose itt, and doe not Stand together for his Glory and your temporall and Divine Liberty that the Lord hath given you.

G: ff.

The 25th of the 5th Mo. 1672
In Rhode Island[1]

1. For Thomas Olney, Jr., and John Whipple, Jr., from George Fox, July 25, 1672 (RIHS, MSS), I, no. 26, p. 18.

APPENDIX III

RHODE ISLAND MERCHANTS

1636–1690

THIS list has been compiled from the sources cited in this volume, principally from the land evidences, where the name of each man was followed by the designation "Merchant." Each merchant is listed in the decade in which his name first appears in these sources; most of the merchants were still in business at the close of the period. They are all Newporters unless it is otherwise noted.

1636–1650

William Brenton
Jeremiah (Jeremy) Clarke
John Throgmorton, Providence
Henry Walton, Portsmouth
William Withington

1651–1660

Francis Brinley
Walter Clarke
Ralph Earle
Robert Moone, Portsmouth
Peleg Sanford
Richard Smith, Cocumscussoc
Laed Streng, "free merchant," formerly New Amsterdam

1661–1670

Nicholas Davis, formerly of Hyannis
William Field, Providence
John Garde
Edward Lecke
Benjamin Newbury
Thomas Richardson
William Richardson
William Sanford
Thomas Ward
Stephen Paine, Rehoboth

1671–1680

John Almy, Portsmouth
Oliver Arnold
Josiah Arnold
Henry Bull
John Champlin, "late of Fayall," 1675
Capt. Thomas Clarke, "Ironmonger"
Thomas Coddington
John Coggeshall, Jr.
Joseph Cooke
Richard Dingley
————Dyer
Thomas Gould
John Hedley
Nathaniel Johnson
Isaac Layton
Israel Napthali (first Sephardic Jewish merchant)
Walter Newbury, "late of London"
Benjamin Rawlins
Richard Smith, formerly of Cocumscussoc, now of Newport
Nathaniel Sylvester, Shelter Island & Newport

John Walley (Whalley), Bristol
Andrew Willett

1681–1690

Weston Clarke
John Coddington, Jr.
William Edwards, Providence
John Greene
Noel Mew
Dr. John Rodman, from Barbados, Block Island
Edward Shippen, from Boston, about 1688
John Whipple, Providence

APPENDIX IV

RHODE ISLAND ARTISANS

AND TRADESMEN

1638–1690

THIS list is far from definitive; it has been compiled from the sources used in preparing this work, especially the several volumes of land evidences. The crafts listed are those used following the names of the artisans who were involved in some kind of transactions concerning land.

ARTISANS

1.	1638	Nicholas Easton, Newport, tanner and miller
2.	1638	John Lutner, Newport, carpenter
3.	1638/9	Richard Maxon, Portsmouth, blacksmith
4.	1638/9	Richard Iles, Aquidneck, carpenter
5.	1639	John Wilbore (Wilbur), Newport, sawyer
6.	1639	Ralph Earle, Newport, sawyer, carpenter
7.	1640	William Withington, Portsmouth, carpenter
8.	1640	Owen Williams, Portsmouth, apprenticed at about age 15 to no. 7
9.	1641/2	William Heavens (Havens), Newport, carpenter
10.	1641/2	John Rome, Newport, house carpenter
11.	1641/2	Thomas Applegate, Newport, weaver
12.	1642	James Rogers, Newport, joiner
13.	1643	Thomas Roberts, Newport, carpenter
14.	1643	John Horndall, Newport, carpenter
15.	1646	Robert Bennett, Newport, tailor
16.	1646	John West, Newport, house carpenter

17.	1646	David Greenman, Newport, wheelwright
18.	1649	Henry Hobson, Newport, carpenter
19.	1649	John Swallow, Newport, clothworker
20.	1651	William Cunygrave, Newport, merchant tailor
21.	1652	John Smith, Providence, mason
22.	1654	"Mr. White," Warwick, bridgebuilder
23.	1655	Thomas Valeston, Newport, cooper
24.	1655	Thomas Olney, Providence, tanner
25.	1656	_____, Newport, distiller "at the Strong Water House"
26.	1656	Edward Greenman, Newport, wheelwright
27.	1657/8	Anthony Lowe, Warwick, wheelwright
28.	1658/9	James Badcock (Babcock?), Portsmouth, blacksmith
29.	1659	William Costin, Narragansett, carpenter
30.	1661	Richard Harte, Portsmouth, leather dresser
31.	1662	William Clarke, Portsmouth, ship carpenter
32.	1662	Richard Dunn, Newport, cordwainer
33.	1663	George Renwick, Newport, leather dresser
34.	1664	Lawrence Turner, Newport, mason
35.	1666	Henry Fowler, Providence, blacksmith
36.	1666	Mathew West, Newport, tailor
37.	-1667	Richard Morris, Portsmouth, gunsmith
38.	1667	William Corey, Portsmouth, carpenter
39.	1668	John Pearce, Portsmouth, mason
40.	1669	Jeffery Champlin, King's Province, shoemaker
41.	1670	Mahershallalhashbaz Dyer, Newport, "Tobaccohouse"
42.	1670	Thomas Brooke, Portsmouth, leather dresser
43.	1671	John Tripp, Portsmouth, ship carpenter
44.	1671	Roger Baster, Newport, blockmaker
45.	1671	William Carpenter, Pawtuxet, housewright, brought from Amesbury
46.	1671	Robert Hazard, Portsmouth, shipwright

47. 1672/3 Aaron Davis, Newport, mason
48. 1673   Thomas Waterman, Aquidnessett, weaver
49. 1674   John Wood, Portsmouth, weaver
50. 1674   _____, Providence, weaver
51. 1674   Moses Lippitt, Providence, aged 6, weaver's apprentice
52. 1674   William Clarke, Newport, weaver
53. 1675   Edward Inman, Providence, glover
54. 1675/6 _____, Providence, dyer
55. 1676   Mathew Boomer, Newport, cordwainer
56. 1676   Henry Stevens, Newport, blacksmith
57. 1676   Robert Taylor, Newport, ropemaker
58. 1676   William Almy, Newport, maltster
59. 1676   John Reade, Newport, cordwainer
60. 1677   John Hicks, Newport, ship carpenter
61. 1678/9 William Clarke, Newport, ship carpenter
62. 1679   Thomas Hicks, Portsmouth, carpenter
63. 1679   James Badcock (Babcock?), Westerly, blacksmith (see no. 28)
64. 1679/80 Thomas Manchester, Jr., Portsmouth, blacksmith
65. 1680   John Reckes (Rekes?), Newport, blacksmith
66. 1680   Thomas Waite, Portsmouth, tailor
67. 1680   Richard Knight, Portsmouth, weaver
68. 1681   Lawrence Clinton, Newport, brickmaker
69. 1681   Thomas Fry, Newport, glazier
70. 1681   Thomas Murray, Newport, brickmaker
71. 1681   Mathew Grenell, Portsmouth, maltster
72. 1681/2 Edward Freeman, Newport, wheelwright
73. 1682   David Greenman, Jr., Newport, wheelwright
74. 1682   Edward Greenman, Newport, wheelwright
75. 1683   Peter Tolman, Newport, cordwainer
76. 1684   Philip Wharton, Newport, tobacconist (tobacco cutter)
77. 1684   Nathaniel Briggs, Newport, tobacconist

78.	1687	John Holmes, Newport, cordwainer
79.	1687	Daniel King, Prudence Island, shipwright
80.	1687	Philip Wharton, Block Island, tobacconist (see no. 76)
81.	1688	Joseph Barker, Newport, tailor
82.	1688	Robert Fish, Portsmouth, blacksmith
83.	1688	Richard Cadman, Portsmouth, weaver
84.	1688	Thomas Stair, _____, housewright
85.	1688	Ralph Chapman, Newport, shipwright
86.	1688/9	Thomas Fry, Sr., Newport, glazier
87.	1688/9	Thomas Fry, Jr., Newport, glazier
88.	1689	Hugh Mosher, Portsmouth, blacksmith
89.	1690	Arnold Collins, Newport, silversmith
90.	1690	John Odlin, Newport, blacksmith
91.	1693	William Heffernan, Newport, cooper
92.	1693	Henry Hall, Westerly, weaver
93.	1690	William Walton, Newport, blacksmith, apprentice to Odlin, no. 90

TRADESMEN

94.	1638	Nicholas Easton, Newport, miller
95.	1638	Richard Dummer, Portsmouth, miller
96.	1648	Brenton's Newport miller
97.	1655	John Smith, Providence, miller
98.	1660	Thomas Cooke, Sr., Portsmouth, butcher
99.	1665	William Corey, Newport, miller
100.	1665	William Earle, Newport, miller
101.	1671	George Lawton, Newport, miller
102.	1683	William Rickets, Portsmouth, miller

APPENDIX V

EARLY WHALING

OFF RHODE ISLAND

1662

T H E offshore whaling fishery of New England had its beginnings, as far as we know, off Southampton, Long Island, about 1647. News of this activity naturally reached Newport, and sometime between that date and 1662 the fishermen of Narragansett Bay took to vexing Leviathan off Brenton's Reef. Dr. Felix Christian Spörri writes that in March 1662 his ship *Black Horse* anchored at the entrance of the Bay awaiting a favorable wind:

"Just as this was done, I noticed some fishermen pursuing a whale. I took great pleasure in watching them and so pleaded with the captain [Alexander] that he allowed us to take the shallop to observe this business, and see how it was carried on. There were two small fishing-boats, each containing six or seven men. These followed closely in the fish's wake; when it raised its head (in which there is a round hole through which it spouts a great quantity of water a spear-length high into the air and through which it inhales air) they moved up beside it and hurled a harpoon into its body. This harpoon was made like an arrow, four fingers broad, pointed and double-edged, fitted with two barbs (like hooks) and a yard long. The back part of this is hollow; and into this lead is poured to give it weight, and a shaft six to seven feet long is fastened. To the harpoon was fastened a rope a finger-breadth in thickness, which the whale drew out. But when they had let out forty or fifty fathoms of rope after him, they held fast, while he dove toward the bottom to break off the harpoon. As this was impossible he rose again, which fact they noticed by the slack in the line and they drew it in again quickly. The other shallop moved up with another harpoon. As soon as he appeared, they cast it into his body. When he felt this new wound, he turned his head down and raised his tail out of the water and beat about with such violence that it was terrible to behold. The fisherman had enough to do to avoid him. When this was of no avail, he began to swim off and shot away with the two shallops so rapidly that the water was cast over them in a spray. He did not continue this for long, for he was already quite weakened and he soon rose again. The fishermen moved closer with long lances or spears and inflicted innumerable wounds until he grew weaker still and began to spew up blood instead of water. This elated the fishermen, who yelled with joy, for it was a sure sign that the fish was dying. They towed him ashore, greatly pleased, for they had earned more than a whole farm would bring us in an entire year. This fish was fifty-five feet long and sixteen feet high; it had only two fins; the tail was broad. Its blubber was two feet thick; this was cut up and put into casks; from it the train, or whale-oil is later made. The teeth, which are as much as six feet long and saw-like, are the whale-bone which is shipped to us [in Holland]. The vertebrae of the skeleton are used by the inhabitants as chairs. In Amsterdam, in Jan Romporth's Tower, there hangs a skeleton eighteen feet in length; from this one can get an idea of what a huge creature this is."[1]

This is the first detailed account of the dangerous but lucrative offshore whale fishery, which never attained the importance in Rhode Island Sound that it did off the shores of Long Island and Plymouth.

1. Felix Christian Spörri, *Americanische Reiss-beschreibung Nach den Caribes Insslen, Und Neu-Engelland* (Zurich, 1677), 44–45; also translation in *New England Quarterly*, X, 544–45. Copy of the original in JCB. The Town of Westerly voted in 1687 that all drift whales cast on shore should be theirs after the king's rights had been seen to. Westerly Town Records, 1669–1713 in Marchant MSS (RIHS), 56–57.

INDEX

INDEX

Agricultural surpluses, 21, 26, 69, 93, 130

Agriculture, 17; development in R.I., 14, 22, 27–29; multicrop system, 28–29. *See also* Crops; Farms; Stock farming

Alcock, Dr. John, 43

Alcoholic beverages. *See* Beer; Wines and liquors

Alexander, Capt., 81, 123

Alford, William, 30

Allen, William, 96

Almy, Christopher, 26, 31, 111, 113

Almy, John, 90

Almy, William, 41, 111

Anabaptists, 4

Andrews, Samuel, 98

Andros, Sir Edmund, 65, 72, 80, 82

Anthony, Joseph, 95

Antinomians, 15, 65, 100

Apple orchards, 21, 29. *See also* Cider

Aquidneck, 4, 15, 17, 28; population, 8; settlement of, 39–40. *See also* Newport; Portsmouth

Arnold, Gov. Benedict, 41, 59, 62–63, 65, 96, 98

Arnold, Richard, 74

Arnold, Stephen, 106

Arnold, William, 87

Artisans and tradesmen, 73–84, 140–43. *See also* Building trades; Coopers; Leather workers; Weavers and weaving

Aspinwall, William, 80

Austin, William, 77

Bailey, Richard, 34

Baker, William, 54

Barbados, 97, 116–19. *See also* Trade, with Barbados

Barley, 29

Barnes, Richard, 109

Barns, 20, 39, 40

Barrels. *See* Casks

Barrington (R.I.). *See* Sowams

Baulstone, William, 30, 86, 101

Baxter, Richard, 4

Bayard, Nicholas, 112

Bayard, Peter, 112

Beans, 28

Beare, Henry, 123

Beef, 44, 46, 48

Beer, 29

Belcher, Andrew, 108

Bellingham, Gov. Richard, 118

Blaufeld, Capt., 25

Block Island, 12, 43, 53

Boats, Small, 10–11, 69, 113

Boomer, Mathew, 106

Borden, John, 95

Borden, Joseph, 117–18, 120

Borden, Richard, 55, 117

Boseman, William, 119

Boston (Mass.), 47, 62, 90

Bowen, Jeremiah, 96

Brenton, William, 19, 23, 31, 42, 55, 58, 95, 99, 100, 101, 114, 121

Brinley, Francis, 42, 53, 69, 97

Brookes, Thomas, 52, 90

Brooks, Timothy, 74

Brown, John, 80

Bryer, Joseph, 121

Budd, John, 53

Budd, Thomas, cited, 114

Buffum, Joshua, 97

Building trades, 75

Bulger, Richard, 85

Bull, Henry, 38

Bullivant, Dr. Benjamin, 129

Butter, 45–46

Byfield, Nathaniel, 109

Cadillac, La Mothe, 57

Candles, 47, 73–74

Canoes. See Boats, Small

Canonicus, 11

Carder, Richard, 19

Cargoes, 25, 31, 94–95, 96, 109, 115–16, 120, 121–23

Carpenter, William, 38, 43, 55–56

Carpenters. See Building trades

Carr, Caleb, 86, 94

Carson, John, 111

Cash, 104, 106

Casks, 76

Cattle, 14, 16, 18, 19, 39, 40, 42–45, 48–49; breeds, 44–45; by-products, 47; dairy, 40, 45; exports, 18, 42; marketing, 32; nomenclature, 43 n. 23; registering of earmarks, 42, 85. See also Beef; Drovers; Hides; Livestock, thefts of; Pounds (public)

Champlin, John, 113

Chapman, Ralph, 83, 96

Charles I, 25

Charles II, 5, 70

Charter of Rhode Island. See Rhode Island, government

Cheese, 41, 45

Child, Dr. Robert, cited, 14, 15, 29, 42, 50

Cider, 21, 29

Clarke, Jeremiah (Jeremy), 25

Clarke, Dr. John, 4, 15, 31, 54, 64, 70, 90, 101; Ill Newes from New-England, cited, 5

Clarke, Thomas, 54

Clarke, Gov. Walter, 102

Clemence, Thomas, 37

Climate, 13, 40, 101

Cloth, 56, 77–78

Clothing, 56, 104–5

Cocumscussoc (R.I.), 21

Coddington, William, 7, 10, 12, 15, 18, 23, 27, 30, 38, 100; fire loss, 20; land sold, 76; Quaker interest, 67, 68, 118; stock raising, 42, 50, 51, 58; tenants, 19, 20; cited, 17, 50

Coggeshall, John, 15, 27, 32, 33

Collier, John, 115

Collier, William, 115

Collins, Arnold, 57
Colonists. *See* Settlers, Early
Commerce. *See* Trade
"Common Protestants," 70
Conanicut, 31, 53, 56, 57 *n.* 45;
Containers. *See* Casks
Cooke, John, 35
Cooke, Robert, 47
Cooley, William, cited, 12
Coopers, 76
Coram, Thomas, 83
Corey, William, 35, 36, 75, 78
Corn, Indian, 10, 14, 18, 19, 21, 28,
    29–30, 78
Cotton, John, cited, 6
Craftsmen. *See* Artisans and trades-
    men
Cranberries, 95
Crime. *See* Livestock, thefts of
Crops, 21, 28–29. *See also* names of
    specific crops
Crossman, Robert, 83
Cudworth, James, cited, 64, 65

Dairies, 45
Davis, Nicholas, 66–67, 112, 117, 123
Deering, Mary, 106
Dexter, Gregory, 75, 87; cited, 5
Dexter, John, 75
Dominion of New England, 72, 92,
    97, 102, 121, 128
Drainage of land. *See* Land, drain-
    age
Drayton, Michael, cited, 29
Drisius, Samuel, cited, 3
Drovers, 86–87, 90, 91, 92
Dudley, Joseph, 72, 128
Dudley, Gov. Thomas, cited, 5
Dury, Andrew, 82

Dutch Island, 10
Dutch traders, 10
Dyer, William, 12, 26, 34
Dyer Island, 12

Earle, Ralph, 35, 38
Earle, William, 95
East Greenwich (R.I.), 44
East Hampton (L.I.), 53
Easton, Gov. Nicholas, 67
Ebbling, Jeronimus, 112
Eddy, Zachariah, 80
Edge, Richard, 98
English grass. *See* Hay and hayseed
European goods, 25, 40, 104, 109

Fairfield, John, 20
Farm buildings, 38, 39, 44. *See also*
    Barns; Dairies
Farmers: gentlemen, 17, 42; small,
    28. *See also* Tenant farmers
Farms: great, 15, 18, 20; small, 20–
    21
"Fat Mutton and Liberty of Con-
    science," 4
Fences, 20, 34–35
Ferries, 84–86
Fertilizers, 16, 30
Fires, 20, 47
Fish, 9, 16
Fishers Island, 17, 25, 32, 50
Flax, 29, 56
Flour, 31
Folger, Peter, 35–36
Food and diet, 14, 29, 46. *See also*
    Beef; Venison
Forests, 13, 16, 22. *See also* Wood
Forret, James, 24
Fox, George, 38, 67–69, 135–36

Freeman, Edward, 42
Friends. *See* Quakers
Fuel, 73

Garde, William, 98, 115
Gardner, Peter, 26, 30, 31
Garious (Garriad, Gariardy,
    Gerard), John, 23
Gentry, 104–5. *See also* Farmers,
    gentlemen; Merchants
Goats, 19, 39, 41, 42
Gold and silver, 105, 106. *See also*
    Cash
Gorton, Thomas, 24, 84
Gould, Daniel, 96, 121
Gould, Jeremy, 19, 20, 50
Goulding, Penelope, 41
Grazing lands, 12, 31
Greene, John, Jr., 23
Grove, Joseph, 120, 122

Hammersmith Farm, 19, 55
Hands, Mark, 117
Harding, Robert, 18, 19, 27
Harris, Toleration, 43
Harris, William, 38, 97; cited, 55, 59,
    70, 77, 80–81
Harrison, James, 82
Hartlib, Samuel, 14
Hawkins, Thomas, 52, 90
Hay and hayseed, 21, 31–33
Hazard, Robert, 106
Hedges, 35
Heffernan, William, 49, 76
Heraldry of the meadows. *See* Cattle,
    registering of earmarks; Sheep,
    registering of earmarks
Herbert, John, 99
Hides, 47, 78. *See also* Leather goods
Higginson, John, cited, 52, 56

Hog Island, 31, 40
Hogs, 11, 18, 21, 39, 40–41. *See also*
    Pork
Holden, Randall, 95, 116
Holliman, Ezekiel, 23
Hooton, Oliver, 119, 120–21
Horn breaking, 47
Horses, 39, 40, 49, 57–59; exports,
    58, 66, 115, 120, 123–24
House furnishings, 36
Houses, x, 75; first shelters, 36–37;
    mansions, 37–38, 119; rebuilding
    of, 37–38, 75
Howland, John, 90
Hubbard, William, cited, 33
Hull, John, 41, 47, 48–49, 59, 110,
    123
Hutchinson, Anne, 8, 10, 21, 66
Hutchinson, Edward, 15
Hutchinson, Eliakim, 54
Hutchinson, Elisha, 54
Hutchinson, Samuel, 54, 91
Hutchinson, William, 15
Hutt, Daniel, 99

Imports. *See* European goods; Wines
    and liquors
Indian wars, 21, 37, 43–44
Indians, 10, 11, 13, 40–41; aid to
    colonists, 10, 11, 16, 17, 28. *See also*
    Canonicus; King Philip; Narra-
    gansetts; Pequots; Wampanoags
Iron, 78–80
Isaac, Arent, 23
Islands, 12, 13, 15–17, 40, 44, 56.
    See also names of specific islands

James II, 102
Jansen, Jan, 115
Jeaffreson, Christopher, 124

Jenckes, Joseph, 74, 79, 80
Jones, Philip, 91
Josselyn, John, cited, 3, 57

Keith, George, cited, 70, 73
Kilvert, Roger, 58
King Philip, 40
Kingston (R.I.), 44, 59
Knight, Sarah, 36

Land: clearing, 19, 28, 35; distribution, 20; drainage, 18, 33; holdings, 21, 133–34; purchases from Indians, 11; transactions, 106
LaRoque, Robert, 113
Laws of Oléron, 24, 97
Lawton, Thomas, 21
Lawyers and litigation, 24, 97–99
Leather goods, 47
Leather workers, 78
Leonard, Henry, 79
Leonard, James, 79
Leverett, John, 87
Leveridge, Richard, cited, 47
Liberty of conscience, 4, 5. *See also* Religious freedom; Toleration
Limestone, 37, 87
Lippitt, Moses, 77
Livestock, 12, 16, 39, 60; exports, 122–23, 124; imposts on, 91–92; marketing, 84, 85, 90–91, 104; portage, 84–85; thefts of, 78, 85. *See also* Stock farming, and names of specific animals
Lloyd, Philip, 98
Long Island, 44, 52, 53
Lovelace, Gov. Francis, 67

Maize. *See* Corn, Indian
Manhattan surrendered by Dutch, 104

Mansions. *See* Houses
Manton, Shadrack, 77
Manufactures, 56, 77–80
Marshall, Timothy, 121
Masons. *See* Building trades
Massachusetts charter vacated, 72, 92. *See also* Rhode Island, relations with Mass.
Mather, Cotton, cited, 4
Mather, Increase, cited, 44
Maverick, Samuel, cited, 59–60, 79, 89
Megapolensis, Johannes, cited, 3
Melyn, Cornelis, 23
Merchants, 71–72, 93–94, 96, 108, 137–39; dealings with mariners and shipowners, 99; Quaker, 70, 96, 109–10, 112
Michele, Thomas, 99
Milk, 45
Minor, Thomas, 58
Minvielle, Gabriel, 112
Moody, Sir Henry, 4, 6
Moors, John, 115
Morris, Lewis, 68
Morton, Joseph, 114
Mun, Thomas, 22
Mutton, 106, 113

Nails, 47
Narragansett Bay, 101–2, 111–12
Narragansett Country, 21
Narragansett planters, 44, 129–30
Narragansetts, 10, 14, 21
Naval office, Newport, 103
Neat cattle. *See* Cattle
New England Confederation. *See* United Colonies of New England
New London (Conn.), 82. *See also* Pequot

New Shoreham. *See* Block Island
Newbury, Benjamin, 109, 121
Newbury, Walter, 96, 105, 110, 113, 114, 119, 120, 121, 124
Newport (R.I.), 13, 23–24, 25, 31, 38, 43, 46, 70, 100, 101, 102, 110, 129; founding, 11, 12, 18; mills, 78; population, 73; seal of, xi, 57; wharves, 95–96
Nicholas, William, 116

Oats, 29, 30
Oldham, John, 10, 11 *n*. 3
Oxen, 19, 20, 46

Paine, Stephen, 26, 96
Palmer, Thomas, 111
Parke, Richard, 40
Parker, Jonathan, 109
Parker, Ralph, 31
Parkes, Henry, 24
Parrott, Simon, 96
Patience Island, 40
Peacock, William, 86–87
Pearce, John, 75
Peas, 28, 30
Peirce, Capt. William, 10; cited, 12
Pequot (New London, Conn.), 25
Pequot Trail, 88
Pequots, 10
Perry, Elizabeth, 110
Pettaquamscutt Purchase, 48, 59, 61, 76, 88
Philip, King of Wampanoags. *See* King Philip
Phillipse, Frederick, 112, 113
Pietersen, Abraham, 10
Pigs. *See* Hogs
Plymouth Colony, 64
Pocasset. *See* Portsmouth (R.I.)

Population, 8, 13, 73
Pork, 41
Portsmouth (R.I.), 11, 24, 34, 42, 43, 44, 54, 55, 59, 78, 84, 85, 100
Potter, Cuthbert, 88
Potter, George, 98
Potter, Robert, 98
Potts, John, 112
Pounds (public), 43
Prentice, John, 111
Prents, John, 111
Privateers, 25, 100, 105
Providence (R.I.), 4, 46
Prudence Island, 11, 40
Pumpkins, 28
Puritans, 7
Pynchon, John, 54

Quaker network: commercial, 66, 69, 70–72, 96, 99, 104, 107–10, 112–16, 119; religious, 67, 68–69
Quakers, 3, 6, 62–70, 103–4, 127; converts, 65; emigrate from Barbados, 62, 117–18; in government, 65, 72, 100; improve roads, 90; meetings & proselyting, 66–69, 70; ministers & public Friends, 73; social programs, 68, 135–36
Quetensis. *See* Dutch Island

Randolph, Edward, 103; cited, 21, 105
Rayment, Richard, 52
Raynham Forge, 79
Read, John, 106
Reape, Sarah, 119
Rehoboth (Mass.), 82, 91
Religion, 4. *See also* "Common Protestants"; Liberty of conscience; Puritans; Secularism; Toleration

Religious freedom, 72

Rhode Island, 3–4, 7–8, 59–60, 128–29; economic growth, 93, 103–7, 127; founding & settlement, 8, 9, 15; government, 5, 90–91; relations with Mass., 25–26, 62–64, 103–4, 106–8; topography & description, 9, 12–13, 16. *See also* Islands; Narragansett Bay

Richardson, John, 114

Richardson, Thomas, 66, 100, 107, 112, 114, 117, 123

Richardson, William, 107, 112, 113, 114, 116, 117, 119, 123

Richman, John, 38

Rivers, 9, 12

Roads, 10, 86–90

Robinson, John, 113

Robinson, Thomas, 24

Rochester. *See* Kingston (R.I.)

Rodman, Dr. Thomas, 121

Rum, 114

Russell, Ralph, 79

Rye, 29

Saffin, John, 108

Salt, 48

Sander, Richard, 120

Sandwich (Mass.), 64, 66

Sanford, John, 15, 52, 84

Sanford, Peleg, 91, 94, 110, 117, 122, 123; cited, 37, 80, 95, 120

Sanford, Samuel, 54

Sanford, William, 80, 95, 110, 117, 124

Sawmills, 74, 79

Scarborough, Edmund, 115

Scott, John, 74

Seals, Official, xi, 24, 57, 57 *n.* 45

Seamen, 24, 100–101

Secularism, 5, 8

Selleck, David, 19, 26

Servants, Indentured, 20, 28

Settlers, Early, 13–14, 15, 27, 39

Sewall, Samuel, 91

Shapleigh, Nicholas, 66, 108

Shawomet (Somerset in Mass.), 82. *See also* Warwick (R.I.)

Sheep, 14, 17, 39, 49–56, 114; marketing, 90; nomenclature, 50 *n.* 34; registering of earmarks, 53

Shelter Island, 25, 67–68

Shipbuilding, 80–84; refitting of, 98

Shippen, Edward, 65, 96, 108, 109, 110

Shipping, 11, 24–35, 56, 69, 84, 112, 115–16, 121; regulation of, 102–3, 121. *See also* Cargoes; Lawyers and litigation; Trade; Travel and transportation

Ship's protests, 24, 98–99

Ships, 25, 81–82, 83, 118–19. *See also* Boats, Small

Shipwrights, 83

Sisson, George, 35

Skillington, Thomas, 115

Skipwith, George, 115

Slave trade, 24–25, 108–9

Smith, John, 74–78

Smith, Leonard, 96

Smith, Richard, 21, 45, 69; cited, 82

Smuggling, 101

Soap, 47

Society of Friends. *See* Quakers

Sowams (Barrington, R.I.), 10

Standish, Capt. Myles, 10

Stock farming, 16, 17, 18, 19, 39–49, 59–60. *See also* Grazing lands; Livestock

Stoddard, Anthony, 109

Stone walls, 35

Storehouse Point, 12

Strengs, Laed, 69

Surpluses. *See* Agricultural sur-
pluses

Sutherland, Mathew, 24

Swine. *See* Hogs

Tallow, 47, 48–49

Tanners. *See* Leather workers

Tar, 73

Taunton (Mass.), 48–49, 79, 80, 83,
89

Taverns, 100

Taxes: excise, 101; local & provincial,
30, 41, 44; port duties, 103

Taylor, Robert, 20

Tenant farmers, 18–20, 28, 35–36,
48–49

Terry, Thomas, 41–48

Thatcher, Thomas, 56

Theft. *See* Livestock, thefts of

Thorn, Edward, 124

Throgmorton, John, 23, 25, 32, 40,
116

Thurston, Edward, 19

Tillinghast, Pardon, 95

Tobacco, 14, 25, 30–31, 98, 114–15

Toleration, 5, 62–65. *See also* Liberty
of conscience; Religious freedom

Trade, 23, 24, 30, 60, 101, 104, 107,
112–18, 120; with Barbados, 18, 41,
42, 58, 66, 97, 110, 116–18; with
Boston, 109–10, 111; in Chesa-
peake area, 104, 114–15; coastal,
23, 25–26, 30–31, 41–42, 66, 69,
104, 110–11, 113–14; favorable bal-
ance of, 103, 104–5; freedom of,
72, 90–91, 92; with Holland, 56,
57, 66; Mass. restrictions on that
of R.I., 64, 91–92; with New
Netherland, 23, 58, 61, 66, 100;
with New York, 104, 112; with
Plymouth, 64; with Virginia, 66;
with West Indies, 24, 25, 41, 42,
73, 104, 120, 121–22

Tradesmen. *See* Artisans and trades-
men

Travel and transportation, 10–11, 85,
88–90, 116. *See also* Boats, Small;
Ships

Tripp, Abiel, 95

Tripp, John, 35

Turnips, 29

Uncas, 11

Underhill, Capt. John, 22

United Colonies of New England, 5,
6, 62–64, 65, 72

Usher, John, 108

Usher, John, Jr., 88

Valenstone, Thomas, 76

Van der Donck, Adriaen, 44–45, 56

Vane, Sir Henry, cited, 5

Van Tright, Gerrit, 112

Venison, 17

Venner, Samuel, 119

Wampanoags, 14, 28, 41

Ward, Thomas, 34

Warehouses, 94, 95

Warner, John, 23

Warren, William, 108

Wars, 26, 100; losses in, 21, 37, 43–44,
55, 74–75, 79. *See also* Indian
wars

Warwick (Shawomet, R.I.), 101

Water mills, 30, 78. *See also* Windmills

Wayte, Joseph, 45

Wealth, 93, 105, 127

Weavers and weaving, 56, 57, 77

Wells, Joseph, 81

Welstead, William, 108, 109

West, Bartholomew, 90

West, John, 38

West India Company, 10, 113

Whaling, 144–45

Wharton, Edward, 66

Wharves, 95

Wheat, 29

Wheelwright, John, 66

Whetcombe, James, 108

Whipple, John, 96, 97

Whittenden Forge, 79

Wild, Joseph. *See* Wise, Joseph

Wilkinson, William, 124–26

Williams, John, cited, 48

Williams, Providence, 41, 110

Williams, Robert, 32, 33

Williams, Roger, 4, 7, 8, 10, 11, 15,
26, 32, 40, 42; cited, 11, 25, 26, 86, 87

Wilson, Samuel, cited, 114

Wilton, David, 54

Windmills, 30, 78

Wine trade, 112, 113

Wines and liquors, 101. *See also* Beer

Winslow, Edward, cited, 34

Winthrop, Fitz-John, 82

Winthrop, John, Sr., 7, 8, 11, 40

Winthrop, John, Jr., 7, 25, 32, 41;
letters received, 17, 25, 26, 50, 51, 86, 87, 119; cited, 30

Winthrop, Samuel, 68

Wise, Joseph, 86, 87

Withington, William, 18, 24, 25

Wolves, 16–17

Wood, 13, 34, 38, 74, 75. *See also* Forests

Woodbridge, John, Jr., cited, 3–4

Woodenware, 76

Woodworking, 73, 74

Wool, 56–57, 77–78, 97, 113–14

Young, William, 98

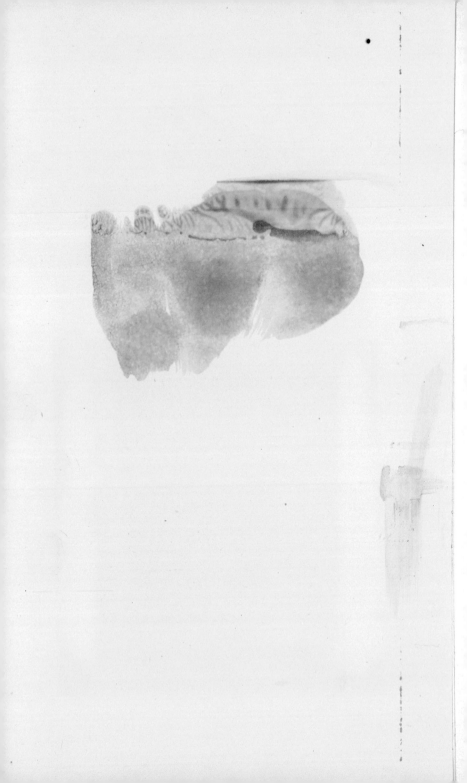